A. J. ROGERS III

With nasty but brilliant comments by FRANK P. BESAG

THE ECONOMICS
OF CRIME

The Dryden Press
901 North Elm Street
Hinsdale, Illinois 60521

To the residents of the Wisconsin State Prison at Waupun for whom crime is no scholastic exercise

Preface

If economic principles are worth their salt, then the logic they embody should help in analyzing virtually any problem involving choice. Behavior which society has defined as illegal certainly involves such choices, and this book attempts to apply the tools of economic thought to the several areas of criminal action.

Anyone who has had either high school economics or a one semester survey course in college will easily handle any of the analytic tools used. For those that haven't been blessed with such a course, a brief appendix of basic concepts is included at the end of the book.

Since economists are always accused of being one-sided and narrow-minded, a sociologist was brought into the act. Frank Besag has provided a few biting comments to leaven the bread. Obviously, I don't agree with many of them; but sociologists and economists seldom do.

Many people contributed to the production of this tome. Arlene Zakhar helped in much of the preparatory work. Many of the cons at Waupun prison helped root out gross errors in the initial draft. In particular, Gary Mason reviewed the draft and gave a good many helpful suggestions. Randy Scott's name should also be included. Finally, Ms Nancy Stein did her usual great job of typing and editing. Any errors remaining are the fault of the publisher who should have known better.

Some day we may have some answers to the problems of crime and punishment. We certainly don't have them at this stage of the game! To get answers, the right questions have to be asked, and economic analysis can at least assist in trying to figure out what those questions really are. No area of human interest is so wrapped up in personal values and morality. There's no problem with this fact as long as the full ramifications of such values and morality are understood and accounted for.

Contents

THE ECONOMICS OF CRIME

CHAPTER 1

An Economist Looks
at Crime

"CRIME doesn't pay!" Now there's a statement that really ought to interest the economist. If it really doesn't pay, why do so many people go into the profession? Is everyone that performs a criminal act a complete nut?

The phenomenon of crime has been with man ever since the beginning. True, what was a crime in one era may not have been judged as such in another time period; but some form of antisocial behavior has plagued man's communities ever since families started living near each other. For a long time, societies reacted to criminal behavior in a fairly straightforward manner. If you didn't obey the rules, you were punished. If you stole a loaf of bread (and got caught), your hands were cut off at the wrists. If you stole a horse, you were hung. If you committed treason or sedition against the sovereign, you were hung, cut down before dead, disemboweled, and drawn and quartered.

There was very little interest in or discussion about the "rights and wrongs" of the crime and punishment system. True, there were always a few kooks who worried about things like moral values and the effectiveness of the existing crime and punishment system. For the most part, however, the average citizen or slave didn't ask too many questions. The poor couldn't afford to take the risks of such behavior and the rich were doing too well to want to rock the boat. The costs and benefits to potential offenders were well established. The offender merely had to weigh the odds of getting caught against the potential benefits of the crime. Institutions from the church to the guilds to the family circle all assisted in adding moral backing both to the law itself and to the punishment meted out to lawbreakers.

In the last few decades, however, more and more people have been asking increasingly embarrassing questions about illegal behavior—its causes, prevention, and punishment. In our world of specialization, the questions themselves and the approaches taken in answering them have tended to fall into the usual ruts of traditional academic disciplines. The psychologist talks in terms of deviant behavior, while the sociologist looks at the characteristics of the community in which crime takes place. Meanwhile, the political scientist examines laws and institutions for answers to the problems posed by crime. And for his part, the anthropologist views the problems in terms of the cultural backgrounds and present mores of the society. Obviously, the economists were going to get into the act sooner or later with their dismal talk of scarcity and cost/benefits. And so they have!

If there is any truth or even consensus in the world, the studies of these different experts should reveal some common thread after all of the trappings of jargon and methodology are brushed aside. Who knows? If the problem becomes serious enough, perhaps we of the separate social disciplines might actually start listening to each other instead of just ourselves. In the meantime, this little book is admittedly parochial. It is one economist's attempt to apply the simplest tools of economic analysis to the facts of criminal behavior. Perhaps some fresh insights can be gained into very ancient problems.

> BESAG: To keep Gus Rogers from being any more parochial than absolutely necessary, I have offered him the aid and comfort of the enemy—namely me, one Frank P. Besag, educator, sociologist, member of governmental commissions, researcher on the school and delinquency problem, and general bon vivant around town. My comments will be distinguished by being set off from the rest of the document so that you may feast upon them without having to read the longer but less brilliant main body of the text.

WHAT IS CRIME?

About the only thing simple about crime is defining it. Crime is anything that is "against the law." All societies have some kind of rules of order. These may represent the consensus of the members of the society or may be established by a single despot. But once these rules are established, breaking them is a crime. This simple definition avoids the much stickier issue of what the rules *should* be or who should establish them. But don't worry, we're not going to sidestep these much more interesting questions. In fact, you will see that the question of what the laws *should be* has a great deal to do with the whole issue of crime.

For his part, the economist is interested and supposedly expert in matters of costs and benefits. How does this interest apply to the definition of crime just presented? If the governing body of a society makes and enforces a law against some particular act, it is obvious that the society and/or its ruling body doesn't like that act. The economist translates "doesn't like" into the idea that such an act would impose *costs*—unreimbursed costs—on the society or ruling body. Take for example a law against sedition—that is, badmouthing the government. Throughout history, such laws have been enforced most actively only when the government itself was in a relatively weak, unpopular, or unstable position. In these cases, talk against the government could easily contribute to its destruction. For the ruling body, this could be a substantial cost for which (to them) there would be no offsetting benefit. Of course, the criminal might be gaining tremendous psychological benefits from speaking his mind; but *from the viewpoint of the lawmaker and enforcer*, the criminal would be gaining this benefit only by imposing serious costs on society's best interests—*as viewed by the lawmaker*.

Take another example in which the government itself is not the injured party. At times, I would gain tremendous psychic benefits from kicking my boss in the behind. My fearless leader, however, would receive no corresponding benefit for this presumably inconvenient and uncomfortable action of mine. True, I could bargain with him ahead of time and pay him the money he would require to suffer the pain and indignity. This would solve the problem of the unreimbursed cost, but it would also take about 90 percent of the fun out of it for me. Given the stated values of this society, I am enjoined by the law from kicking Clyde or anyone else. The law makes a crime out of any action on my part that imposes unreimbursed costs on others. At least, this is the idea behind many laws. But in our imperfect world, it doesn't always work out this way.

Those of you who have studied some economics will recognize these cases as examples of *externalities*. Costs are being generated beyond those imposed immediately on the perpetrator of the act. We are all familiar with other examples of externalities. The coal-burning electric plant is paying for the costs of producing electric energy and receiving benefits in the form of revenues from the sale of that energy. But maybe the smoke from the plant is peeling the paint off half the houses in the neighborhood. This damage is *external* to the market for electric energy. The power company is using the waste disposal capacities of the air without charge. Therefore, the customers using electric power are receiving the energy without bearing the total cost of the product, which includes the cost of any environmental damage.

Benefits, too, can be external to the primary act or process. A typhoid patient will pay for medical services. This payment represents a cost to him and a benefit for those performing the medical services. But over and above this *exchange* of resources, the public at large may benefit from the control or elimination of the disease, which is a potential health threat to all. Here the public benefits from the expenditure of a private individual. One of the biggest rationales for public expenditures—say, on education—involves presumed benefits to the community as a whole *greater than* the sum of the benefits received by individuals who obtain and use the education. If this is true, then public expenditures are clearly justified, *given the position that benefits should be paid for by those receiving them*. This assumption is often ignored, but it's the only thing that makes the statement itself correct.

For its part, crime is only a *subset*—a part of the acts which impose external unreimbursed costs on others. Imposing these costs becomes a crime only when it is *illegal*—against the law of the land. For example, an academician might decide to use the research findings of one of his students to prepare a scholarly article. Further, he might omit biographical credit to the student. If the material has been copyrighted by the student, our scholar is in trouble with the law; but if the student hasn't gotten a copyright, our scholar is *legally* home free. Killing people is another example of how the law views the imposition of external costs differently under different circumstances. If my son decides to shoot me, the law will take a very dim view of his action. On the other hand, the law of the same community might result in his receiving a medal were he to wipe out a village of people considered to be our "enemies." Substantial unreimbursed costs would be imposed in either instance, but the *law* makes one a crime and the other an heroic act of battle.

There are any number of ways that criminal acts could be classified. For this book, the quite arbitrary breakdown of crimes against persons, crimes against property, and crimes without victims will be used. It is true that these categories overlap considerably, and this fact will be discussed as well. The crimes against persons include murder, assault, manslaughter, and forcible rape. Property crimes include larceny of all types, plus vandalism and fraud. Crimes without victims are those such as drug use, alcoholism, prostitution, gambling, and obscenity. For the purposes of analysis, this breakdown will assist in getting at some essential differences in the cost/benefit structures leading to and resulting from these crimes. Society's reaction to criminals and their acts will be analyzed by using a simple cost/benefit analysis. Hopefully, some of the costs which society incurs when reacting to criminal acts will also be made explicit by this approach.

CRIMINAL STATISTICS

Getting statistics on most behavioral situations is hard enough, but obtaining useful data on criminal activity is even tougher. On a nationwide basis, the main source of information comes from the *Uniform Crime Reports,* published annually by the Federal Bureau of Investigation. This compilation of numbers about criminal activity and law enforcement leaves a great deal to be desired. It is based upon voluntarily supplied information from local law enforcement agencies. Only crimes *reported* to these agencies are included—not the total number of occurrences. "Major" crimes become part of a category called *Crime Index Offenses,* and these receive more detailed analysis. Murder, non-negligent manslaughter, forcible rape, robbery, aggravated assault, burglary, larceny over $50, and auto theft comprise these offenses. Other crimes are reported as well and are broken down by everything from sex to age.

> BESAG: I think the distinction between "petty" and "major" crimes is not a reasonable one. Many crimes which could really be considered petty are dealt with rather harshly—particularly property crimes. Yet the Billy Sol Estes types do not need to fear serious consequences much more than the person who writes his second bad check for $35.00. Further, many crimes which are of little overall cost to the society are dealt with very harshly indeed. For example, murder affects very few people—far less than graft, for example—but it is treated very harshly. Sex crimes are extremely rare, and (as is the case with murder) are not prevented by fear of punishment; but in the state of Wisconsin, sex criminals are given, for all practical purposes, indeterminant sentences.
>
> Perhaps a better distinction than "petty" and "major" would be to differentiate between those crimes that have a high emotional content at a particular time, as opposed to those that do not. This emotional content will change from time to time and place to place. Being called a communist by Joseph McCarthy in the 1950's had far more serious consequences than stealing from the government or your own campaign fund. During some

periods, murder will be high on the list; at others, welfare cheating will head the top. The point to remember is that the "objective seriousness" of the crime is less important than the emotional content in predicting the seriousness of the consequences. It should also be pointed out that the rulers are entirely capable of using their powers to shape the feelings of the masses so that they will be more emotional about some types of crime than about others—*e.g.*, witness the present administration's "law and order" push and the way that the statistics and the media have been used to make it a major issue. At present, the Law Enforcement Assistance Administration (omnibus Crime Bill of 1968) has more money to spend on "research" than the Office of Education has for their whole budget.

Crime is on the increase. Even the most optimistic observer cannot deny this fact. The degree of the increase is another question, and here is an interesting use of the FBI numbers. Figures 1.1, 1.2, and 1.3 show the FBI charts of crime increase from 1960 to 1970. The total reported and verified crimes as well as the rate per 100,000 of population are presented for total *Crime Index Offenses,* index crimes of violence, and index crimes against property. On a raw basis, the percentage increases are indeed phenomenal. Total index crimes reported and verified rose 176 percent; index crimes of violence, 156 percent; and index crimes against property, 180 percent. Clearly, population was increasing during the period; so it would be better to look at the rate per 100,000 of population. This cuts the increase down somewhat to 144 percent, 126 percent, and 147 percent respectively.

However, in checking the back of the FBI's book (Tables 24 through 28), we find that the number of agencies reporting in 1960 was 2,528, while the reports for 1970 came from no less than 5,270 agencies—over twice as many! This increase in the number of agencies reporting represents an increase in the reporting base, not an increase in the crimes actually committed. On the other hand, if the reports made in 1960 and 1970 by the same

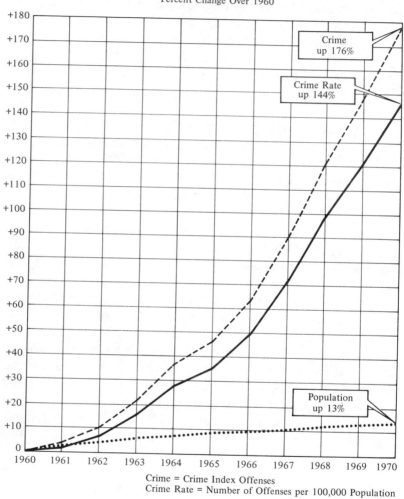

CRIME AND POPULATION
1960 - 1970
Percent Change Over 1960

Crime = Crime Index Offenses
Crime Rate = Number of Offenses per 100,000 Population

Source: FBI, *Uniform Crime Reports, 1970*

Figure 1.1

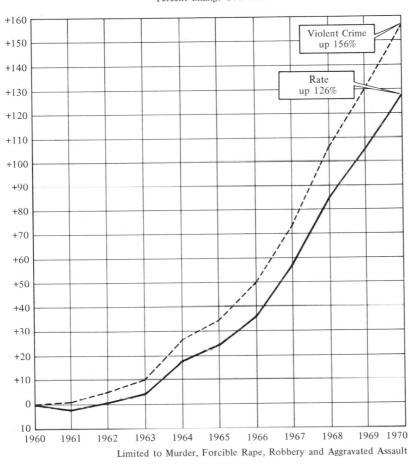

CRIMES OF VIOLENCE
1960 - 1970
Percent Change Over 1960

Limited to Murder, Forcible Rape, Robbery and Aggravated Assault

Source: FBI, *Uniform Crime Reports, 1970*

Figure 1.2

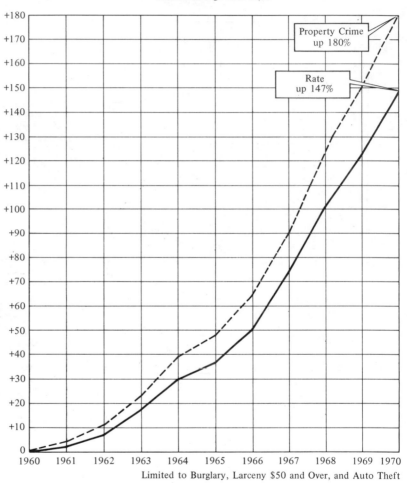

CRIMES AGAINST PROPERTY
1960 - 1970
Percent Change Over 1960

Property Crime
up 180%

Rate
up 147%

Limited to Burglary, Larceny $50 and Over, and Auto Theft

Source: FBI, *Uniform Crime Reports, 1970*

Figure 1.3

agencies are compared, a slightly different picture emerges. Total crime reported and verified (not just *Index Offenses*) rose by 31 percent in agencies reporting in both 1960 and 1970. Index crimes rose by 86 percent, consisting of an increase of 87 percent in index property crimes and 83 percent in index crimes of violence. Nobody suggests that this increase is insignificant, but it is a bit less panic-producing than the bold figures that made the headlines.

Anyway, crime is certainly important enough to merit our serious study. This book is constructed so that even if your training in economics is negligible up to this point, you should be able to plow through the material with relatively little difficulty. Most of the relevant concepts are reviewed both with and without the usual geometry of simple economic analysis.

Probably most of you have already had a basic course in economics. This will be the assumption on which the rest of the book is based. However, realistically, we all know that you don't remember much about those lousy supply and demand curves or the theory they were supposed to represent. Anyway, there is an appendix at the end of the book that should help you review some of the more important basics. Putting it back there probably means that most of you won't even glance at it; but it's there, and it will be referred to several times throughout the rest of the book. It's your choice whether you use it or not.

CHAPTER 2

Crimes Against Persons

IT was Thursday afternoon and the bloody computer which controlled the operation of half the production line went on the fritz. Joe and 300 other guys were laid off three hours early. Two weeks before Christmas and the paycheck would be short! What a lousy break! As he drove into the parking area behind his duplex, Joe noticed an extra car. It looked like the one that belonged to the unemployed creep who lived several blocks down the street. Joe and Maxine had met him at a big birthday party some weeks before. The s.o.b. was one of those long-haired freaks that the women went for even though he had probably never earned an honest dime in his life. Maxine had had a little too much to drink and this guy had tried to put the make on her, but old Joe had showed him. One good punch had cooled him off.

Joe let himself in the back door. There wasn't a sound on the first floor. Normally he would have slammed the door and yelled for Maxine. But for some reason Joe himself didn't really understand, he kept his mouth shut and climbed the stairs to the second floor. It was as if he himself were wrongfully entering a forbidden area. The silence of the first floor gave way to a soft mixture of male and female sighs, groans, and laughter. Joe did a 180-degree turn and went back down the stairs to a small table in the hallway. From a drawer in the table, he took an army surplus .45 semiautomatic and very deliberately walked up the stairs again. This time he didn't even pause. Throwing open the bedroom door, he aimed at the topmost bare body. The .45 slug entered the right side of the freak's neck and blasted out through the top of his head. A bloody Maxine was still screaming when the cops arrived half an hour later. Joe was sitting downstairs in the living room—just sitting—and they took him away.

CRIMINAL STATISTICS

Sounds just like the latest soap opera, doesn't it? The problem is that about 71 percent of all murders in 1970 were committed within family groups or resulted from arguments among people who knew each other. Only 20 percent of the murders were committed as part of a known felony, although another 9 percent took place in connection with suspected felonies. There are no figures which would indicate just how many of these were truly "premeditated" and how many were crimes of momentary passion, but estimates are that by far the largest portion resulted from a fit of passion or a sudden rage.

> BESAG: Many murders which are not crimes of passion are still not really premeditated acts, but are in fact incidental to the commission of another crime. For example, the law assumes that anyone who carries a weapon during the commission of a felony is planning on using it. For this reason, a killing committed during an armed robbery is considered premeditated murder—even if the assailant kills the victim with the victim's weapon. Although statistics are almost impossible to get, pure murder seems to be a relatively rare crime.
>
> To make this somewhat clearer, let us look at the number of murderers in the state of Wisconsin. In 1970, 7.3 percent of all incarcerated inmates were murderers. This seems like a pretty high percentage until you realize that of all those prisoners released in the same year only 1.7 percent were murderers. Further, murderers are rarely given probation (returned to the community under the supervision of a probation officer without serving

time in prison). There were none given probation in Wisconsin between January of 1968 and December of 1969.

Perhaps most striking is the murderer's length of stay in an institution. While the average criminal stays in prison for 19.6 months, the murderer stays in prison for 78.7 months! Under these circumstances, the 7.3 percent figure of all inmates listed above should really be reduced to about 2 percent, since each of the murderers stays in prison four times as long as the average inmate.

The point of this discussion is that premeditated murder is a fairly rare crime—not because the penalty is high, but because the return on the investment is low. Murder for profit just isn't profitable. There isn't enough money in it. Murder for emotional, instantaneous, and transitory return (it resolves our conflict, makes us feel revenged momentarily, etc.) is profitable; and regardless of the price, the perpetrator will still buy the crime.

Like murder, aggravated assault takes place most of the time within a family group or among people who know each other. An accurate breakdown of this phenomenon is not available. But clearly the problems of prevention and deterrence are very different for those crimes which result from momentary passion than for those which take place on a planned and calculated basis. This latter category should probably be analyzed in at least two subgroups. One would consist of murders or assaults committed in accordance with certain preplanning. The other sub-group would consist of murders and assaults committed as a contingency to another felony. For example, the problem of a planned gangland killing, an assigned contract, or a beating that a loan shark purposely gives a client certainly pose a different prevention and deterrence problem than the beating or murder that happens "accidentally" during an armed robbery or other criminal action. This is not to say that one is more serious than the other, but rather that the methods one might employ to inhibit this category of crime effectively would vary considerably.

There are some other FBI numbers from the *Uniform Crime*

Reports-1970 which might be of interest at this point. Figure 2.1a shows the percentage of murders committed with various weapons, and Figure 2.1b shows the circumstances under which murders were committed. Figure 2.2 shows the breakdown of weapons used for aggravated assault as a percentage of the total acts. These numbers will be referred to as this discussion progresses, but it would be useful if you got a general idea of their magnitude as you read the upcoming paragraphs.

Forcible rape is the final category of crimes against persons. As defined by the FBI crime report figures, forcible rape includes any "carnal knowledge of a female through the use of force or threat of force." Assaults to commit forcible rape are also included in the numbers, but statutory rape without the use of force is excluded. This category made up less than 1 percent of the index crimes in 1970 and only 5 percent of the total crimes of violence. Nevertheless, it will be included in this discussion because of the differences in costs and benefits it embodies for criminal, victim, and society.

BESAG: It is interesting to note that the FBI indicates that rape can only be committed on a female, although there have been some interesting cases of late where a man has reported having been forced to have intercourse with a female or a group of females. In all of those cases, however, the man involved seemed to be bragging more than complaining. It seems that in our society rape is a purely male offense: if it is committed on a male, he should enjoy it; if it is committed on a female, she should not. So much for male chauvinism.

On the other hand, it should be pointed out that taking indecent liberties with a child is almost always a male crime, since females are expected to fondle children while males are not. There are, in brief, no dirty old ladies. So much for female chauvinism.

Frivolous—although accurate—comments aside, it is important that we understand that sex crimes are

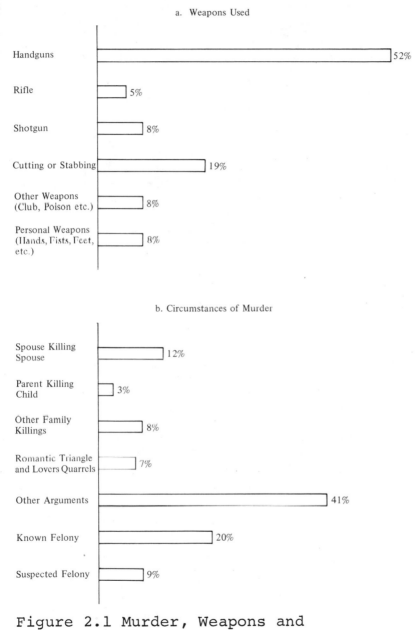

a. Weapons Used

Handguns 52%

Rifle 5%

Shotgun 8%

Cutting or Stabbing 19%

Other Weapons
(Club, Poison etc.) 8%

Personal Weapons
(Hands, Fists, Feet,
etc.) 8%

b. Circumstances of Murder

Spouse Killing
Spouse 12%

Parent Killing
Child 3%

Other Family
Killings 8%

Romantic Triangle
and Lovers Quarrels 7%

Other Arguments 41%

Known Felony 20%

Suspected Felony 9%

Figure 2.1 Murder, Weapons and
Circumstances

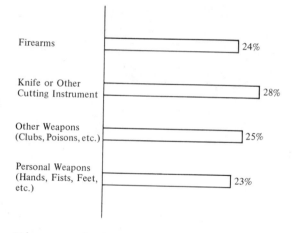

Figure 2.2 Aggravated Assault by Type of Weapon Used

extremely emotional and that they receive far more publicity than is warranted by the statistics. Rape and attempted rape involved only 2.5 percent of the inmates (all male by the way) in Wisconsin incarceratory institutions. Indecent behavior with a child involved only 2.1 percent of all the inmates (again all males). Happily, the state of Wisconsin has finally moved sex offenses out of the incarceratory division and into the division of mental health; therefore, therapy rather than social protection becomes the prime concern.

As with murder, the length of stay at the institution for sex crimes is much higher than for other crimes. As stated before, the average length of stay for all inmates in Wisconsin is 19.6 months. The average stay for those convicted of rape is 50.2 months. For those convicted of indecent behavior with a child, it is 26.8 months. (This relatively low figure may be due to the fact that indecent liberties with a child can quite literally include anything from patting a child on the bottom to rape.) The point here is that the 2.5 percent figure (percentage of inmates convicted of rape) may be too high for interpretive purposes, since those convicted of rape stay in prison over twice as long as the average inmate.

As a sidelight, you will notice that I never used the term "rapist" or "child molester." It is easier to get convicted for these offenses than for many others because of the emotional content of the crime. In more cases than we would care to admit, the child or woman victim turns out to be emotionally disturbed and the alleged criminal behavior never to have occurred at all. For example, every year in Whitefish Bay, a suburban area of Milwaukee, the police turn out a ghastly little brochure about a pony who protects little darlings from dirty old men who might molest them. The general tone of the document is that no child should ever speak to anyone; and that if anyone speaks to the child, there is only one possible reason—namely, molestation. The child is warned that he or she should immediately report anyone who says hello to them to their parents who, in turn, should report it to the police. I became enraged at the brochure and phoned the police to ask how many cases of child molestation there had been during the last two years. I was told that there had been none. When I asked how many cases had been investigated, I was told that there had been about 15. I then asked when the cases had occurred; and, lo and behold, I discovered that they had been reported and investigated and dismissed right after the ghastly brochure had been distributed. It would appear to me that since they had little else to do in the suburban district, the police had decided to drum up some business for themselves.

Two points are important: (1) although children are taught very early that sex deviates are a great danger, they, in fact, are not; there just aren't very many of them. (2) If YOU, dear reader, are ever accused of being a child molester, you will have one hell of a time getting out of it; the population as a whole thinks that sex crimes are rampant, and that anyone accused of a sex crime must be guilty because the victim said so.

MURDERS OF PASSION

So much for the statistics. Our purpose here is to apply some basic analysis to the criminal act and its potential punishment. To begin with, let's consider the act of murder. Specifically, let's talk about the act that is not committed for pure material gain but rather as an act of passion or other emotional behavior. Society establishes a penalty for this kind of action; it can range from a few months in prison to execution. The reasons for establishing the penalty in the first place can be a combination of at least four different motives, and these apply to other criminal offenses as well. They include the desire to *deter* an act, to gain *retribution* for an act, to *protect* against similar acts by the same person (incarceration), and/or to bring about *rehabilitation*.

If we start by looking at the deterrence factor, we are immediately confronted by the standard arguments for and against capital punishment. These arguments continue to rage, and there is clearly no definitive empirical evidence to substantiate either view. What's more, it is questionable whether *truly* definitive evidence could be obtained under any circumstances. However, we can look at the assumptions of the people who feel that increasing penalties—including the death penalty—will successfully reduce the incidence of murder. This group is saying, in effect, that the potential murderers have a *demand* for murder which is similar to the demand function for less bizarre goods and services. In other words, the quantity of murders demanded (and, in this case, generally supplied by the demander himself) will be greater if the price of the murder is low, and smaller if the price of the murder is high.

Price, of course, is used in its broadest (and correct) sense: it is the total package that must be sacrificed by an individual for one unit of the desired good—in this case, one murder. For the moment, we are not considering murders by third parties for hire. This will come up in a short while. Right now we're talking about the do-it-yourself murderer. Since most criminal acts involve an "act now, pay later" situation, the price is *not* a specific thing which is known in advance with perfect certainty. In other words, the price in our demand function is actually an *expected price* based on the knowledge and information of the offender.

Figure 2.3 illustrates this kind of a demand for murder function (DD). As the expected price is increased, the quantity of murders demanded (and, in this instance, supplied by the do-it-yourselfers) will decrease. The expected price could include length of imprisonment, hard labor, fines, lack of sex life, or death itself. In this particular case, however, the price is not set by the interaction of supply and demand forces. At least in the short run, the price is set by the governing body and courts of the community; and it is set at any moment in time without regard to the quantity of murders. In other words, the mandatory sentence

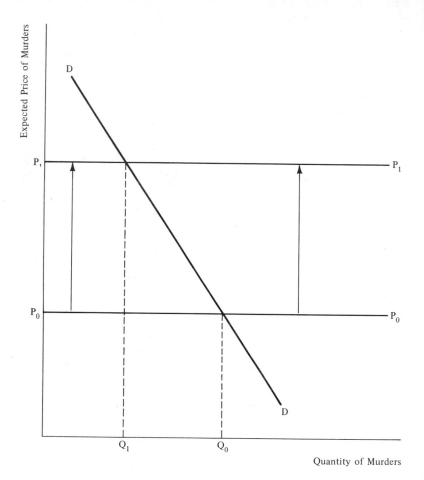

Figure 2.3 The Demand and Price for
         Murder

for first degree murder would be 20 years without possible parole. This is the sentence per murder regardless of the number of murders committed in any particular day. True, if the murder rate increased dramatically, there would probably be a large hue and cry to *raise* the price, but this would be a change over time rather than a function at any moment in time.

Figure 2.3 illustrates such a shift from price P_0 to P_1. Here the assumption of the deterrence crowd becomes clear. If the price to the potential demander (and, again in this case, the supplier) is raised, there will be a significant reduction in the quantity performed. The quantity in this case will be reduced from Q_0 to Q_1. For the economists in the audience, this assumption merely states that the demand for murder will be sufficiently elastic for the quantity to respond "significantly" to change in price.

Let's go back to the little vignette at the beginning of this chapter. On a "normal" day in Joe's life, what do you suppose his demand for murder function looked like? Assuming he was like most people, he would view murder as a *negative good*. In other words, instead of being willing to *pay* some positive price to commit murder, he normally would have required substantial *payment* to do so. You may object that most people's price would be infinitely high to commit such a crime, but I doubt this. The fact that men fight and kill in wars—even wars they don't believe in—would lead me to think that most men's price to commit murder is considerably lower than most of us care to admit.

In Figure 2.3, the demand for murder function was drawn as a demand curve for a positive good. Figure 2.4 shows a demand curve for a negative good. Demand DD begins at a negative expected price. Instead of being willing to pay to get the murder done (or commit it oneself), one would require payment to be enticed into committing the act. The slope of DD indicates that as the positive price was raised, (negative price reduced) the individual would be more willing to commit murder.

Assuming this was Joe's demand for murder function before the crime, everyone was safe as far as Joe's harming them was concerned. But the moment he caught his wife in bed with the other man, Joe's demand function changed greatly. Not only did

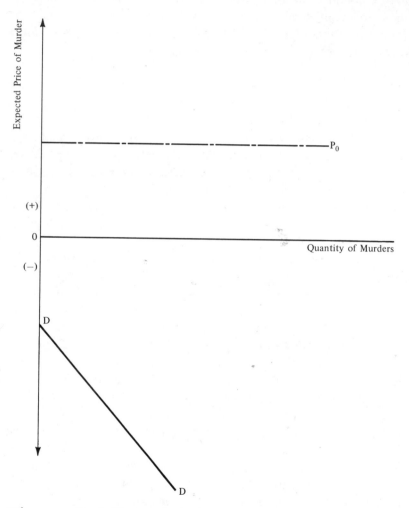

Figure 2.4 Normal Demand for Murder
          Function

the act of murder become a positive good (the curve moved from the negative quadrant into the positive quadrant), but the passion of the moment also made the demand for the act independent of the expected price that society might extract later.

Figure 2.5 illustrates the situation graphically. Demand DD shifted to D^1D^1, which is now not only a positive demand but also a completely inelastic one. Regardless of the expected price of committing the murder, Joe was going to do it. Quantity Q_0 was the murder of the other man, no more and no less. If the expected price had been higher, say P_1 instead of P_0, the quantity demanded would have remained the same. Later, after Joe had been convicted and sentenced to 20 years in prison, he told his lawyer that the penalty for committing murder had never entered his mind when he had carried out the act. That's what Figure 2.5 indicates.

> BESAG: Murder is a lot like suicide in that it is usually not heavily premeditated although it is often thought about. What happens in suicide is that things get to be too much and the person figures he might as well end it all. If he has to think about it too long, however, the chances are that he will either decide against it or will do a bad job of it and be "rescued."
>
> The timing in both murder and suicide is very important. The desire to end it all for yourself or some one else must come at the same time as the ability to commit the act; otherwise the desire will go away. Pills, high buildings, bridges, handguns, etc., must be there when you feel like committing suicide.
>
> If you should fail in a suicide attempt, you may be sent to prison or a mental institution, since many states still have laws which make suicide a crime. This price is of little or no concern to the "criminal", however. In point of fact, he may look forward to the punishment as the expiation of some guilt.
>
> The same timing factor holds true for murder. In crimes of passion, if the ability to murder is not present

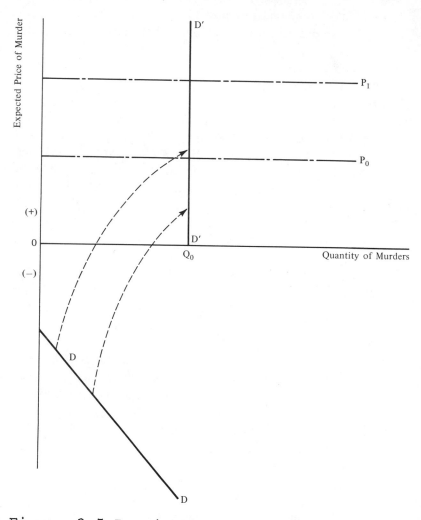

Figure 2.5 Passion and the Demand for
Murder

at the same time as the passion, there will be no murder. If Joe had not had a gun handy, it would have been more difficult to kill the other man; he would either have had to beat him to death or knife him to death, both of which are more difficult and more personal. In murders committed as part of a felony, most would not have occurred had guns not been available either to the criminal or the victim (the victim's gun is often used against him).

The guilt expiation factor is also a part of the murder-out-of-passion syndrome. The murderer often stays at the scene and freely confesses his crime—often over the objections of the district attorney, who doesn't want a confession without a defense lawyer being there.

In brief, not only must the potential suicide and the murderer usually be paid heavily for their crime—either through the supposed end of suffering, or revenge, or guilt—but the means to commit the act must be present at the same time as the desire. Price is not the object, timing is.

If the deterrence factor of punishment for Joe's type of violent crime doesn't operate very well, how about the other motives? It is certainly doubtful that prison would "rehabilitate" a guy like Joe. He already had a very marketable skill and committing the crime had nothing to do with his material welfare or lack of it. Protecting society from future acts that might be committed by Joe could be an argument, but there is a good deal of evidence to indicate that Joe would be less likely to do this sort of thing again than most other people. True, were he a psychopathic killer, incarceration and treatment would clearly be in order; but our assumption is that Joe had no such mental problem.

However, if society did not punish criminals to a point that would satisfy the revenge feelings of the sufferers, there might be increasing attempts to "take the law into our own hands." This in turn could lead to a breakdown of the legal system and all of the incumbent costs such a breakdown would precipitate. To many people, this argument for retribution would seem very weak.

People *shouldn't require* retribution. It runs afoul of most moral codes. Perhaps so; but given the present state of man's nature, retribution seems to be a very human desire and one that cannot just be sluffed off as improper.

If it is true that usual deterrence methods are comparatively ineffectual in combating passion murders, what measures might be implemented to reduce this category of crime? Since passion is a transitory emotion in most people, anything that would make the murder act more time-consuming and require more personal involvement could reasonably be expected to improve the chances of cooling off the would-be murderer before the deed was done. The figures presented earlier on the weapons used in murder might give a clue to one way that the act could be made more difficult. Handguns accounted for over 50 percent of all murders; firearms of all kinds accounted for more than 65 percent. Again, there are reasons to believe that these figures are low and that guns accounted for an even larger percentage of murders. The use of a gun is comparatively simple and impersonal. No body contact is required, and there need be no direct confrontation between victim and murderer. The process is extremely fast and requires little or no physical effort.

> BESAG: Firearm murders also require damned little skill. That becomes important not only from the standpoint of murder, but also if you happen to be an innocent bystander when some idiot comes in and starts shooting up the bar, restaurant, party, or sauna in which you happen, by chance, to be. Professional murderers don't scare me. Idiots with guns do. I never go anywhere during deer hunting season, and I try to stay out of dear hunting season altogether.

Certainly no one can prove that reducing the firearms in the community would necessarily reduce murders of passion, but there is certainly a great weight of informed opinion which indicates that this would indeed be the case. One all-too-popular bumper sticker running around the country announces that when guns are outlawed, only outlaws will have guns. From the standpoint of committing murder, this would be an improvement over the present situation, since most of the murders in the country are not committed by criminals.

MURDER FOR PROFIT

The business of murder for fun and profit is clearly not one of the major industries in this country. However, it does exist, and its analysis provides an interesting contrast to the murder-for-passion example just discussed. In this case, we have an actual market operating, albeit small and imperfect. The demand for the service of murder is now matched with a supply provided by either individual entrepreneurs or, more generally, a service organization which maintains an operating staff of killers. The price of murder will now be an actual dollar amount, derived from the interaction of supply and demand in any particular murder market. Figure 2.6 shows such a market.

For comparison purposes, we will assume that the market in Figure 2.6 is operating legally, and that it is perfectly legitimate to hire the services of a murderer if you want someone killed. This doesn't necessarily mean that it is a *morally* accepted practice, but merely that the *law* does not prohibit or inhibit such a course of action. As with any other good, as the price of murder services decreases, the cost of the services derived from this good decreases *relative* to other alternatives. Alternatives might include coercion, or just plain putting up with the bum. As the relative price of this good decreases, the quantity demanded increases; and we end up with a demand curve such as DD. This analysis and the analysis of murder from passion have the same looking demand curve; but in the previous case, the prices were the *expected* prices in total terms. Now the prices are in terms of money. These money prices will tend to capture all of the other expected costs of buying a murder, such as expectations of getting caught, pangs of conscience, etc.

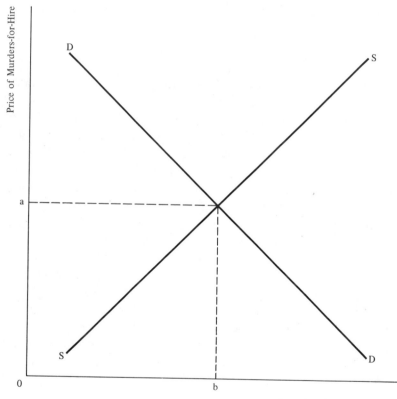

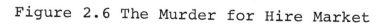

Figure 2.6 The Murder for Hire Market

BESAG: There was a time when murder was relatively legal; namely, during the 1920s and early 1930s with Chicago's Murder Incorporated. A number of interesting things happened which would appear to follow the traditional market model. First of all, Murder Incorporated had to cut down (no pun intended) the competition so that they could corner the market and set prices. They also had to establish certain norms for their own behavior. (Once a contract had been let it was carried to completion regardless of a higher price which might be offered by the victim; the maker of the contract was not revealed nor was the person who carried it out.)

All of this led to the professionalization of murder. Amateurs were discouraged and sometimes eliminated when they got in the way. The result was that the total number of murders actually decreased during the existence of Murder Incorporated. In fact, because of the probability that rival contracts would be let, plus the fact that many enemies had been eliminated, the price became so high that Murder Incorporated priced itself out of the market.

The main difference in the two murder analyses is in the supply side of the question. The murder-from-passion example assumed that the demanders were also the suppliers of the service. There was 100 percent interdependence between supply and demand. The price was set by the imposed will of the community operating through the legal machinery. In the murder-for-hire case, there is a regular supply of murder services; and the supply curve shown in Figure 2.6 assumes that as the price of murder services increases, the quantity of services available will increase. Potential murderers' attitudes toward the act itself and their alternative employment possibilities are implicit in the rising supply function. As the relative return for performing murder services rises vis-à-vis alternative earning possibilities, larger numbers of murderers will come forth to supply the service.

The market price and equilibrium quantity are shown in

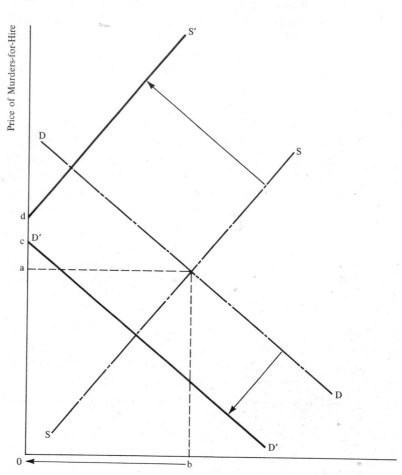

Figure 2.7 The Murder for Hire Market

Figure 2.6 as 0a and 0b respectively. This price and quantity combination and only this price and quantity combination will "clear the market." Remember that at this stage of the game, we are still assuming that the act is legal. All of the usual competitive assumptions of perfect information and lack of monopolistic powers are also assumed. Now let's see what happens when these highly unrealistic assumptions are dropped one by one.

First of all, what is the intended impact of a law prohibiting some given behavior? In terms of our market analysis, the answer is clear. A prohibiting law is intended to work on both the demand and the supply of the illegal service. If the law is completely successful, demand and supply will both be cut back as shown in Figure 2.7. Now the *lowest* price at which anyone is willing to provide the service is greater than the *highest* price anyone is willing to pay for it. Demand curve DD has been reduced to D'D', while the supply function has been cut back from SS to S'S'. The lowest price at which any supplier is willing to provide the murder service is 0d. The highest price anyone is willing to pay for the murder service is 0c. Since 0d is greater than 0c, there will be no murder services performed.

What things in the supply and demand functions are actually changed by imposing the law? On the supply side, the *costs* of providing the services have been increased. Now there is a penalty which might range from a monetary fine to execution *if* the supplier is caught carrying out his profession. But it is one thing to establish a law and a penalty for violating the law, and quite another thing to *enforce* it. Enforcement requires the expenditure of resources. In most societies, the large majority of laws require such enforcement resources or costs. If a penalty for murder was established, but no enforcement was carried out, there would be little change in the supply function. The *effective* change in costs as viewed by the hired killer would change very little if at all. As more and more resources are expended on enforcement, however, the *expectations* of getting caught also increase. Only when this happens does the existence of the penalty have any effect on the supply of the criminal service.

BESAG: One of the factors that led to the demise of Murder Incorporated was the increased expectation that the buyer would be caught. It turned out that keeping the contractor's name secret was almost impossible. But there was no necessity for going through the bothersome business of a court trial; rather you could adopt the relatively simple procedure of letting out a contract on the person who had let out a contract on you. As a result of this practice, the price (namely death) went up for the first contractor, and he decided that maybe he ought not to engage the services of Murder Incorporated after all.

None of this holds for the passion murder or the murder committed during the commission of a felony. Here the price is no object, because the murder was not intended or planned or really thought about. In these murders, timing is the important factor, not price.

On the demand side of the market, the establishment of a law prohibiting the act in question works on two variables in the demand function. First of all, the law appeals to people's sense of community. There is at least some incentive for people to obey the law because it is the "right" thing to do. In our demand function, the enactment of a law against an act reduces the "taste" for that act. But the most important impact on taste comes from another fact. Under the law, the demanders of many criminal services can find themselves judged equally guilty as the suppliers of the service. In most communities, buying murder services would make the buyer as guilty as the murderer himself. Again, because of this potential cost to the *demander*, his taste for the service will likely be decreased with the resulting decrease in demand. As with the supplier, the likelihood of getting caught will be the real deterrent, not the existence of the penalty per se.

The second impact on the demand function is closely related. Making the service illegal means that the costs of obtaining market information on the parts of both supplier and demander will increase. Since information about the market is potentially dangerous, elaborate and therefore expensive precautions must be taken by both contracting parties. By the same token, the contracting process itself will also be made much more expensive by the illegality and potential penalty attached to the act. For the supplier, these facts will tend to shift the supply curve back (to the left) while demand will also be reduced.

Laws generally do *not* eliminate the illegal act. Instead of shifting both supply and demand back to the desirable positions illustrated in Figure 2.7, the more general situation is for supply and demand to be reduced to a point that will still permit some amount of the illegal activity to take place. In Figure 2.8, such a situation is shown, using our example of hired murder. Without the law, the free market would result in 0b murders being committed at a price of 0a per murder. Imposing the law reduces both supply and demand from SS and DD to S'S' and D'D' respectively. Since the supply is reduced more than the demand, the new market price has been raised from the free market level 0a to 0c. (Notice that if the demand for the illegal service were to be reduced more than the supply, the market price would actually fall rather than rise.) The quantity of murders committed has fallen from 0b to the new level at 0d. The law has been partially effective since bd fewer murders are now being committed. However, only if further steps are taken to decrease supply and/or demand to an even greater extent will the illegal act actually be eliminated from society.

This chapter has been dealing primarily with crimes of violence. The examples used have been murder from passion and murder for material gain. The analyses are similar for other crimes involving bodily harm. Assaults are motivated both from outbursts of passion and for material benefit. For this category of violent crime, the same analyses apply exactly, although the seriousness of the crime is probably less to both victim and perpetrator. Forcible rape involves another set of motives, and results in a different set of costs and benefits to the offender. But a combination of the analyses used in describing crimes of passion and crimes for profit can be used to describe this act as well.

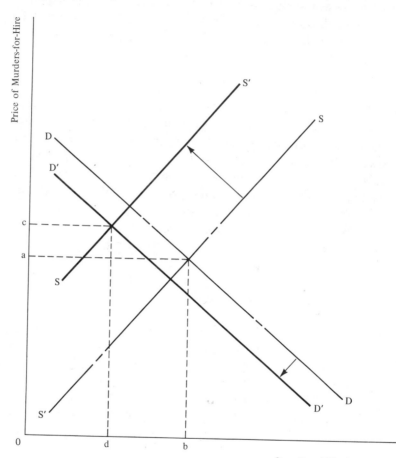

Figure 2.8 The Murder for Hire Market–
          Imperfect Control

BESAG: It should always be remembered that most crimes of violence are really accidents that occur because of other things. If Joe had not come home that afternoon, or if his wife had been smart enough or cautious enough not to adulterate at home, the murder would not have been committed. Similarly, in the case of an armed robber who kills his victim, if the robber had not had a gun, or if he had not been nervous, or if the victim had not been fed up with getting robbed so often and had not wrestled with the robber, or if the victim had not had a gun which was taken from him by the robber, the murder would not have been committed. The price for armed robbery (length of jail sentence) is higher than for robbery and that is why many robbers do not carry weapons. Those who do, however, clearly do so because they are afraid that they will be killed by the victim (a higher price than a longer jail sentence) who often has a gun and no compunctions about killing an unarmed robber. It is entirely possible that one reason for the increase in armed robbery is that the victims have armed themselves, thereby increasing their resources and the price which must be paid by the robber: therefore, the robber feels that he must get an "equalizer" to decrease the potential cost to himself while increasing the cost of resistance to the victim. The critical factor seems to be the ease with which people can get guns.

CHAPTER 3

Crimes Against Property

IN the Appendix to this book, there is a brief discussion of property rights and their relationship to the whole problem of scarcity and the allocation process. Essentially, if property rights are not defined and enforced, there can be no systematic allocation of any good produced from scarce resources. Any crime against property is an attempt to gain some bundle of property rights over some particular good without paying the usual costs. The purse snatcher grabs a handbag, runs away to evade capture and punishment, and hopes that the bag over which he now has control contains negotiable resources. The embezzler juggles the company's books to allow the taking of company assets without normal compensation. The armed robber merely reinforces his ability to take from others by increasing his victim's potential cost of noncooperation.

All illegal acts which involve unreimbursed transfer of property rights from a legal holder to an illegal holder have serious impacts on society as well as on the individuals concerned. In a sense, such acts tend to destroy the whole structure of property rights by subverting the normal conditions for exchange. In Chapter 5 there will be a discussion of who pays what for property crimes, but here we will discuss the *kinds* of costs generated by this criminal activity.

CRIMES AGAINST PRODUCERS

There is a philosophy among some people today which holds that ripping off the people and businesses supplying goods and services to the community is somehow okay. After all, these money-hungry bums are ripping off the consumers every day, so any property crime against them is merely a form of social justice. Let's see how property crimes against suppliers actually work.

In the Appendix the factors that influence the quantity of any good supplied are enumerated. All these factors have something to do with the *costs* of producing the commodity concerned. Higher cost factors mean that a smaller quantity of the good will be produced at any given market price.

As an example, let's take the department store industry in a particular location. The product that firms in this industry are selling is the warehousing and merchandising of a variety of goods and services. Their costs consist of depreciation on buildings and equipment, labor in the form of sales personnel and clerical staff, cost of the merchandise stocked for sale, plus capital, maintenance, and utility items. Let's establish this industry in the middle of an isolated community whose members belong to a religious sect with one very strange tenet. They believe that to steal merchandise from retail stores is a mortal sin roughly equivalent to mass murder. This belief is so ingrained in the populace that enforcing a no-stealing policy requires very few resources. A good sharp meat axe is kept handy to draw and quarter anyone whose morals slip, but this really doesn't happen all that often.

Because of this condition in the community, the stores in the retail industry have no requirement whatsoever for guards or police forces. Furthermore, they don't even require burglar alarms or expensive locking systems on their doors. Of course, the community isn't terribly prosperous, so the industry doesn't set any sales records. But they don't have a pilfering problem. In Figure 3.1, we have illustrated the market for retailing services provided by the retail industry in this area. We are assuming a competitive industry in which no one firm controls the prices of the services, but this assumption is not critical to the analysis.

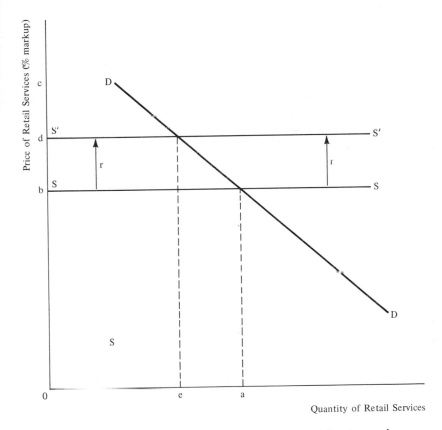

Figure 3.1 The Market for Retail Services

The supply curve of retail services is horizontal, indicating that increased levels of service could be provided without higher per unit prices for the services. In other words, it is assumed that true economies or diseconomies of scale do not exist. The demand for retail services again illustrates the law of demand under which larger quantities are demanded at lower prices, everything else being equal. The price of the product in this case would actually be the margin added to the cost of the goods sold by the department store from which the store's costs (including normal profit) are paid. Under our idyllic circumstances, market equilibrium would be attained at a quantity of retail services equal to 0a and a price of 0b.

Now let's assume that the community goes to hell. Expansion of a nearby metropolis has caused a lot of strange middle-class types to displace the original settlers. For ease of analysis, we will assume that there is no change in their demand for retail services compared to the demand of the previous customers. But there is one major change. The new group doesn't have the same hangups about pilfering. As a matter of fact, they view shoplifting as some kind of game to be played as much as possible. The first impact on the store is a decrease in the amount of money received for goods as compared to the amount paid out to wholesalers for goods. For every 20 pairs of stockings actually sold, one pair is swiped. For every 100 pairs of shoes sold, five pairs walk out of the store without reimbursement. This means that about 5 percent of the value of their *gross sales* is going out the door without being paid for. Assume that the average merchandise costs the store 20 percent less than their selling price. In other words, a $100 piece of furniture costs the store $80. If the pilfering rate (based on retail value) equals 5 percent, this means that one quarter of the store's operating revenues are being ripped off. In most retail operations, this 5 percent pilfering loss would exceed their net profits.

How then can the store stay in business? In a competitive situation, if just one store were being pilfered, that store would be forced out of business. But if all of the stores in the marketing area are having the same problem, then this loss will be added to the costs of doing business. This add-on might come from one or both of two cost additions. First, the *effective* cost of the merchandise they actually sell has increased by the wholesale value of the stolen goods. (For the numbers crowd this raises the cost variable argument in the supply function.) But, also, the store will probably look for means of reducing the pilfering. Security systems of one kind or another will be implemented, using personnel, alarms, dogs, closed circuit TV, or other *policing* devices. This raises one category of the supplier's transactions costs —*policing costs*. The effect of either one of these two cost additions is to reduce the quantity of retail services supplied for any given level of retail service price. The supply curve of the industry is shifted proportionally upwards as with S'S' in Figure 3.1.

The vertical distance of the shift (r representing ripoff costs) is the actual increase in the per unit costs caused by the pilfering. In Figure 3.1, this increase is shown as though it were the same for any level of output. The industry is facing a proportional ripoff regardless of their volume of business.

Does all of this mean that the customers are going to pay the full increase in the pilfering costs? The answer is maybe yes and maybe (more likely) no. As can be seen in Figure 3.1, the degree of the impact on the customers' price (and the stores' selling price) will depend on the *elasticity* of supply and demand for retail services. If an increase in the price of retail services causes a substantial proportional decrease in the quantity of those services demanded, then suppliers themselves are going to bear a portion of the costs. In essence, some of the higher cost operations in the industry will simply have to go out of business. More efficient firms will absorb part of the increase from profits; and customers will pay a higher price, but will not foot the bill for the full increase. In the diagram, the total increase in costs equals r. If all of this increase were absorbed by a price increase, the price would rise from 0b to 0c. But because the demand in this case is quite price responsive, the price only rises to 0d, while the quantity marketed falls from 0a to 0e.

BESAG: It may be that who absorbs the price is to some extent determined by who did the shoplifting. Let's just take three different kinds of shoplifters: kids who do it either because it is fun or because they want the particular item and don't have the money to buy it; kleptomaniacs who theoretically can't help themselves; and politico-shoplifters who do it because they don't see ripping off the merchandiser as a crime. The first category involves kids of all socioeconomic groups. The second involves largely upper middle and upper socioeconomic groups. In *Social Class and Mental Illness*, Hollingshead and Redlich point out that the lower classes can't afford neuroses and don't have time for them, while the upper classes do have time and can afford them. The same holds true to some extent for kleptomaniacs. The third category involves largely those who either by choice or by circumstances are in the lower income groups and feel cheated by the society in general and the merchandiser in particular.

It can be assumed that the shoplifting done by kids although high in quantity is low in overall quality—that is, it constitutes a low loss to the merchandiser on a per capita basis. However, the cost of shoplifting is passed on to all consumers through higher prices and to the merchandiser in terms of profits not gained and resources spent.

The kleptomaniacs form a small group and are very often protected by a family which has made arrangements with the local merchandiser that all thefts will be covered. In that way, many of the costs are ameliorated before they can be passed on to other consumers or to the retailer.

The third category, however, is of a totally different type. Here the theory of the shoplifter is that his behavior is politically motivated, and he attempts so far as possible to avoid passing the cost of his behavior to his own community. For example, the black political shoplifter attempts to shoplift from those stores which are not locally owned and which must pass the cost of the shoplifting on to other areas. Sears Roebuck, for example, does not attempt to pass the full cost of shoplifting at a particular store on to the consumers of that store only. Rather it distributes the cost to many stores. Further, the black political shoplifter would not shoplift a black-owned store or a black and locally operated store. This political shoplifter is to be distinguished from the pure shoplifter who will shoplift where it is easiest.

The point here is that the cost of shoplifting is distributed unevenly across the population, since the rich must pay for their own shoplifters and the political shoplifters as well.

CRIMES AGAINST DEMANDERS

Referring to variables in a demand function discussed in the Appendix, you will note that *transactions costs* appeared as something affecting the quantity of a commodity demanded as well as the quantity supplied. The way these costs (Information, Contractual, and Policing or *ICP*) affect supply, should be fairly obvious; but we'll go through an example just to make sure the point is understood.

An increase in the crimes against property is likely to have a considerable impact on the demand for the property concerned. Imagine the expected effect of riots in inner city areas on the demand for property within those areas. More specifically, think of the effect on the demand for retail shops. With the increased expectation of violence and vandalism, the costs of operating any retail enterprise are going to rise in much the same way as before. In this instance, however, the shop property is the good being considered and the potential shop owner is the demander of that property. An increase in the potential of violence translates itself directly into some kind of increased cost in maintaining the property rights purchased. Buying the store means that property rights

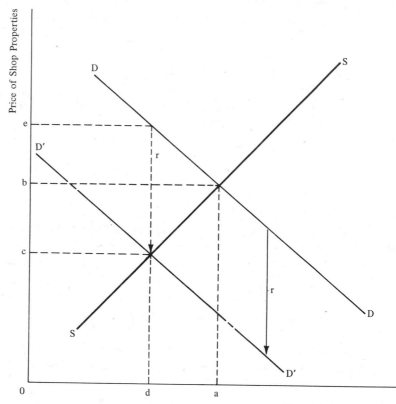

Figure 3.2 The Market for Shop Properties
in the Inner City

are transferred from the previous owner to the demander. These rights are meaningful only as long as they can be enforced. With an increase in anticipated violence, the *cost* of maintaining these rights increases in one or several ways.

First of all, the shopkeeper may decide to install his own protection system in the form of alarms, locks, or guard dogs. A second possibility is for the new (or potential) owner to secure additional, and most likely more expensive, insurance against the variety of property crimes that are now anticipated.

> BESAG: (Or not be able to get insurance at all. This has become a problem in some riot areas where owners have sold out and new merchandisers have not been found because there was no opportunity to insure the property.)

A third alternative is for the community of which the shopkeeper is a member to increase the resources expended on police protection. This will increase the taxes paid by the demander. Any way the pie is cut the *policing costs* of the demanders of shop property will be raised. And as a result, the *demand* for shop properties will be reduced.

In Figure 3.2, this situation is illustrated in a comparable manner to the effect on supply shown in Figure 3.1. Starting from the nonviolence equilibrium with a price of 0b and a market quantity of 0a, suddenly the cost of ownership of this property is increased by the amount r. Actually measuring the increased cost of ownership is a problem, since this cost would somehow have to be amortized over the expected useful life of the property. But, conceptually, it is easy to see that however the potential demanders view this increase in cost, their demand for shop properties will shift downward by a dollar amount equal to r. This time the "ripoff shift" has hit the demand curve instead of the supply curve. But as was the case with the impact on supply, this impact on demand does not mean that the new market price for the properties will drop by the amount of the increase in transactions costs. Part of the ripoff shift will be absorbed by a decrease in the price of the good. But another part of the impact will be absorbed by a reduction in the quantity marketed. Price will fall by bc; but this is not as great as the increase in costs, ec. The equilibrium quantity will fall from 0a to 0d.

Carrying our "mirror image" analysis further, if the quantity of shop properties supplied is completely unrelated to the market price of the properties—if supply is completely inelastic—then the total impact of the ripoff shift would be felt in a lower price. On the other hand, if the supply is completely elastic, the impact would only occur in the form of a reduced quantity marketed.

In this particular example, there might be an erroneous conclusion drawn from the fact that the *price* of shop properties has declined. This might be interpreted to mean that the costs of operating retail establishments have declined, which is certainly not the case. On the contrary, the costs of operation for the shopkeeper have *risen* because of increased probabilities of criminal acts; and, in all likelihood, the prices of the merchandise he sells will also rise in order to cover these increased costs.

THE MARKET FOR RIPOFF PROPERTY—DEMAND

Some property is merely destroyed or damaged out of protest, hatred, or acts of psychosis. But for the most part, property crimes are committed because there is a chance for profit. There are markets for stolen goods just as there are markets for legitimately marketed goods. It is the existence of these markets that makes it possible for thievery to be a thriving business and a viable alternative to other earning possibilities.

In our analysis, let us begin by imagining that one market operates in the country for a single commodity—stolen property. To start with, we will assume the highly unlikely proposition that this market is operating under conditions of perfect competition, which include good market information, freedom of entry and exit, and no particular power concentration in either the supply or demand segments. How can we apply the usual demand function to this market?

First of all, the law of demand states that the quantity of a good demanded will vary inversely with its price. There is certainly no reason to doubt that this is the case for our illegal goods. One would certainly expect that the cheaper the good, the more of it would be demanded, everything else being equal. The degree of this inverse relationship—the elasticity of demand—would depend on the same kinds of variables that would determine the elasticity of demand for legal goods. If there are many substitutes for the illegal good, the demand would tend to be elastic—changes in price would cause comparatively large changes in the quantities demanded. If purchase of the illegal good involved a substantial portion of the demander's budget, then again price changes would bring about relatively large quantity changes. Finally, if the good were a *necessity* in the view of the demander, the demand would tend to be inelastic. In this case, price changes would bring comparatively small changes in the quantity demanded. We'll be talking a good deal more about this last case in the next chapter, which deals with addictive drugs.

The next variable in a demand function is the price of related goods. If the price of a substitute good goes up, the demand for the given good will go up. If the price of a complementary good goes up, the demand for the given good will fall. Whatever substitutes a good might normally have, an *illegal* good always has its *legal* counterpart as a substitute. In Figure 3.3a and 3.3b, we can see how this interaction takes place. In Figure 3.3a, we have shown the supply and demand for scotch whiskey legally imported, taxed, and distributed. In Figure 3.3b, we have shown the supply and demand for stolen scotch whiskey. The only assumption made about both supply curves at this stage of the game is that more quantities will be called forth in either market if the respective product prices rise.

Now assume that the government raises the tax on the legal whiskey by an amount equal to t in Figure 3.3a. This shifts the supply curve of the legal stuff from S_wS_w, to $S_{w'}S_{w'}$. In the other market, the demand for illegal scotch was constructed holding the prices of all possible substitutes constant. Among these substitutes, of course, is legal scotch. The increase in the tax, t, has raised the price of legal scotch from 0c to 0d. Since the price of a legal

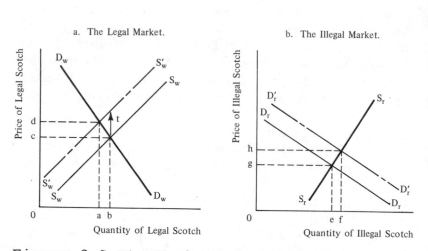

a. The Legal Market.   b. The Illegal Market.

Figure 3.3 The Markets for Scotch
             Whiskey

substitute has been raised, the *demand* for the illegal product will be increased from D_rD_r to $D_{r'}D_{r'}$. This will both raise the price and the equilibrium quantity of illegal goods.

The opposite reaction can be expected in the case of complementary goods. For example, if the *price* of automobiles increases, one would expect that the *demand* for hot tires, hubcaps, and other accessories would decrease.

How about the effect of income changes on the demand for illegal goods? As with the legal goods, there are undoubtedly those specific hot goods for which increases in demanders' incomes would cause a decrease in demand (inferior goods). Other illegal merchandise would find better markets if the demanders' incomes increased (normal or superior goods). There is probably one income effect that could be expected in a general sort of way. To the extent that there are penalties imposed on purchasers of stolen goods who get caught, it is probable that increased incomes would very likely be accompanied by an increased aversion to legal sanctions such as jail or fines. To the extent that this is the case, stolen goods in general would be inferior goods. Increases in incomes would bring about a greater fear of getting caught and punished by society. Unfortunately, there is another possibility connected with increased incomes and wealth. There is a considerable body of evidence indicating a *negative* correlation between wealth and getting punished even if caught. The true "normalness" or "inferiority" of stolen goods will have to await a great deal more empirical study than has been carried out thus far.

BESAG: There are a number of interesting corollaries to the wealth-buying stolen goods construct. There seems to be some relationship between the amount of wealth and the types of goods bought and the amount one is willing to pay for them. By and large, middle or low income people will buy some luxuries, but will more often buy the semi-luxuries such as cars, refrigerators, TV sets, etc. The wealthy would not buy such items on the black or illegal market under normal circumstances, but would certainly buy items which were scarce. For example, during a wartime rationing period, the rich would still buy specialty food items regardless of the cost, while the poor would only buy those things which were necessities on the black market.

The cost is also affected: while the items which the rich buy illegally are by and large much more expensive than the over-the-counter market (this is true of scalped theater tickets and meat during wartime), the items which the poor buy illegally are by and large cheaper because they are "hot."

Next comes that economist's catchall, tastes. Clearly, demanders' tastes for illegal goods will be an important variable affecting the quantity demanded. The most obvious component of tastes consists of the morals and mores of the buying public. To the extent that people can be convinced that purchasing or otherwise using stolen property is wrong, their tastes for the property will be reduced—thus reducing demand. When morals in this area decrease, the opposite situation takes place; and the demand for hot goods increases. As with any other good, a change in fads can have an impact on the demand for the illegal good. For example, if people cut down on their desires for cigarette smoking, the demand for the legal product and the contraband product will both be reduced. If the people decide to smoke pot *instead of* drinking booze, then the demand for both legal and illegal booze will go down.

Finally, we come to the effect of transactions costs on the demand for illegal goods. As usual, we will break these costs facing the demanders into *I*nformation costs about the product and market, *C*ontracting costs in making the purchase, and *P*olicing costs of maintaining the property rights purchased through the market. One of the serious problems that the seller of illegal goods faces is the difficulty of advertising his product. For example, were he to advertise half-price television sets, it wouldn't be long before somebody started asking embarrassing questions about where those cut-rate television sets came from. This problem of the seller becomes a cost to the potential buyer—an information cost. He must locate a seller of the illegal product through word of mouth or by spending time searching him out. All of this can be resource-consuming, which will decrease the level of demand that would otherwise exist. Looking at the other side of the coin, if information about illegal markets were to become more readily available, one would expect the demand in those markets to increase.

> BESAG: In most cities, the illegal market is pretty well known to both buyers and authorities. It is relatively easy to find out what things are available at what cost, and what the probabilities are that you will be arrested for accepting stolen goods or that the fence will be arrested for selling stolen goods. This will vary from city to city and from time to time. During a crackdown, it would be hazardous both to sell and to buy. During normal periods, it would be hazardous to sell but not to buy. During lax periods, neither would be hazardous.
>
> By and large, the authorities have a pretty good idea of who the fences are and what they are selling. Except in unusual circumstances, it is both too difficult and too expensive in time and money to try to arrest, try, convict, and sentence such a criminal. At present in the state of Wisconsin no one is in prison for selling or receiving stolen goods. Either there aren't very many fences, or they are convicted of other things, or no one is paying much attention.

The process of contracting the exchange of property rights over stolen goods can raise several problems, and thus can potentially generate contracting costs of greater magnitude than would be the case in a legal market. In most cases, it is the moment of transfer of the item that makes the buyer potentially culpable as a receiver of stolen property. Increasing the expectation or possibility of getting nailed while making the purchase effectively increases contracting costs to the demander.

BESAG: As a corollary to the above paragraph, not only are the fences largely known for what and when they sell, but they are also known for the care with which they protect their customers and guarantee their merchandise.

The issue of protecting property rights to the purchased stolen commodities raises some interesting points and problems for the demander. Since the sale itself was illegal in the eyes of the law, protecting the rights acquired by the sale can be a problem. If the good concerned is of relatively low value and lacks any means of specific identification, the chances are that the purchaser would have little or no problem maintaining his control over the item. But if the item is major, like an automobile, and has specific identification possibilities, the purchaser might be hard pressed to push for his "rights" if they are challenged. Even if things like serial numbers are carefully changed on a stolen automobile, the purchaser would probably hesitate before going to the police to report its theft or damage. This continuing problem of maintaining illegally gained property rights undoubtedly has a significant impact on reducing the potential demand for identifiable property. Thieves are well aware of this fact, as is evidenced by the general practice of breaking up identifiable merchandise into smaller and less traceable components. Automobiles are stripped for salable parts rather than being sold as whole units. Even bicycles are stripped and reassembled from different sets of components. All of these actions are attempts to make the stolen property more salable by making it "safer" to own.

THE MARKET FOR RIPOFF PROPERTY—SUPPLY

If you refer to the discussions in the Appendix, you will find that the quantity of any good that people would be willing and able to supply depends upon the price which the potential supplier can receive in the market for the good. At any given market price, the quantity of a good supplied is a function of its cost of production, the technology available for production (really just a special form of costs), and the costs of marketing the good. So it is also for our illegal good market.

First of all, consider the price of the stolen goods and its impact on the quantity of stolen goods supplied to the market. As the price which the supplier can command goes up, there is obviously more incentive for him to increase his efforts to supply additional quantities. Everything else being equal, it is certainly reasonable to assume that the higher the market price for hot goods, the larger will be the quantity supplied.

How about the costs of production for the supplier of hot merchandise? In its simplest form, take the independent operator. He's the guy who does his own thing alone or perhaps with a few chosen associates. He is a professional, but scorns large well organized rings—at least as far as the actual stealing process is concerned. As will be mentioned a bit later, he may use the marketing services provided by a well developed "fencing" operation. So, what are the costs to our independent operator? First of all, if he is anything but a rank amateur, he will have made substantial investments in training costs. Just like the ivy league alumnus, our hero has probably sunk a considerable amount of his time in a training institution where he was able to rub shoulders and absorb wisdom from some of the finest in his field.

> BESAG: By and large, the training he received was better organized, shorter in duration, more direct, and a good deal more usable and salable than its ivy league counterpart. He also has more interest in learning, possibly for the above reasons.

Unlike the case of some ivy leaguers, daddy didn't pay the bill for this training. Instead, it was gained in one of those second order tax-supported institutions called prisons, penitentiaries, correctional institutions, reformatories, etc. The investment made was primarily his *time*. The cost of the investment depended upon just what his alternative earning opportunities might have been on the outside. There is little doubt, however, that time in prison would generally amount to a substantial sum if priced out with even minimal alternative outside wages. In passing it should be noted that John Q. Taxpayer also has a king-sized investment in our friend, since the per capita cost of these institutions generally exceeds that of our finest boarding schools and colleges.

> BESAG: It costs about $500 per month to keep a man in prison in Wisconsin. And the total cost to the state for all incarceratory facilities is slightly more than eight million dollars a year. This is higher than some, since Wisconsin does attempt to maintain a good rehabilitative system. It is lower than others, since Wisconsin tends to be less corrupt than many other states. Of the money spent for prisons, 36.61 percent is used for supervision (guards, etc.), while 17.71 percent is used for rehabilitation and recreation. (There is no separation made between rehabilitation and recreation. That is another example of trying to use budgetary information for program planning. It doesn't work.)
>
> The argument is made that supervision is a 24-hour-a-day, seven-day-a-week affair, while rehabilitation and recreation are carried out only five days a week for eight hours a day. But that is beside the point, because most prisoners are returned to society after about two years (that's high for Wisconsin), and we should be spending our money and time on rehabilitation so ex-convicts won't become recidivists. If prisons force us to spend twice as much on supervision as on rehabilitation and recreation combined, then perhaps there is something wrong with using prisons for rehabilitation. Maybe they should be used only for social protection, and maybe rehabilitation should be carried out in halfway houses, which are not only cheaper (about $250 per inmate per month) but also have a much better record of rehabilitation.
>
> By their own statements, ex-convicts do not use the

official training they receive at the prisons. Of 994 parolees in 1970, 691 (69.5 percent) indicated that they had not used the training they had received in prison; 180 (18.1 percent) said that they had used it, and the remainder fell into the nonapplicable category. The success rate difference between those who used their training and those who did not was only 2.2 percent (62.8 percent vs. 60.6 percent). This would seem to indicate that the official training programs in Wisconsin prisons have little or no effect on the parolees' success (although there may be some carry-over from one training program to all work—*e.g.*, good work habits, etc.). It also says nothing about what an inmate learns informally from other inmates.

As with any graduate, once our hero gets out of stir, his training cost becomes a "sunk" cost. He can't get it back *except* as the investment improves his future earnings flow. Let's look at his alternatives as he walks away from the gray walls. In spite of "enlightened" public opinion and sentiments, a con getting a straight job is going to have a tough time. The better the job in terms of earning power and job conditions, the tougher time he will have getting it. If, at the same time, the labor market is such that jobs are hard to come by, our friend's problem is compounded even further. Most of these better jobs are also going to require further training, which represents an additional investment of his time and other resources.

On the other hand, he is already trained in the business of larceny. The capital requirements to establish his own business are very small. True, there is always the risk of getting caught and sent back to the pen, but every occupation has its hazards. As a very rough idea of what happens, our infamous numbers from the FBI *Crime Reports* show that 63 percent of persons released from prison in 1965 were rearrested within four years. Again, the numbers may be off a great deal, but the story is there. How many Harvard graduates junk their college training to start a new vocation after graduation? Reduce the average income and wealth of the Harvard graduate to bare subsistence and ask the same question again. It is amazing that recidivism figures are not higher!

> BESAG: Recidivism rates have to be looked at with some caution. A distinction has to be made between committing a new crime (real recidivism) and violating parole or probation (phony recidivism). Of all the residents in Wisconsin prisons in December of 1970, 25.3 percent were readmissions—that is, they had been in prison before. The rest were new admissions.
>
> Of the 25.3 percent that were readmissions, 43.5 percent (11 percent of all those in prison) were readmissions without a new sentence—that is, they had not been convicted of a new crime but were parole violators, which could involve the most minor infraction or a major one. Conversely, 56.5 percent of the readmissions (14.3 percent of all those in prison) had committed and been convicted of new offenses. All of this confuses the picture and makes interpretations of recidivism rates very difficult. In any case, real recidivism is not as high in Wisconsin as one would expect.

The impact of technology on our supply of stolen goods function is interesting. As the battle against property crimes escalates, increasingly sophisticated robbery techniques become desirable, if not essential. This sophistication includes greater specialization of functions, greater use of capital equipment, and greater need for protection against interference from the police. All of these factors certainly provide incentives for larger scale operations. The rugged individualist in the stealing business may be forced to go down the tube, as has the small farmer in the agricultural racket. Technology is making it tough for the little guy. Yet to the extent that technological developments in the larceny field reduce the costs of supplying stolen goods, the market supply curve will be increased—shifted to the right. But large scale operations may make the little guy a "subsistence" operation, doomed to poverty and very prone to recapture and reimprisonment.

It is in the last variable of our supply function that potential benefits from large-scale organizations can best be seen. The transactions costs (ICP costs) facing a small operator can be staggering. First of all, he must get *information* about his product to potential demanders. This requires careful merchandising techniques to avoid complications from the law. The actual *contracting* of the sale opens him to the same kinds of risks faced by demanders in exposure and its incumbent costs. The policing costs faced by suppliers are those of the businessman. Policing the supply in this market means expending resources to keep society's police from busting up the operation.

HOW THE MARKET WORKS

At this stage of the game, the analysis is completely simpleminded; and most of it has already been covered in bits and pieces discussed thus far. In Figure 3.4, the supply and demand of stolen goods is drawn. From society's standpoint, the idea is to reduce demand as much as possible and to reduce supply as well. The hope is to accomplish the "perfect law," where supply price is greater than demand price at zero market quantity. This was discussed in the last chapter. Realistically, society hopes to reduce the volume of traffic in this market substantially. They are trying to arrive at some lower level of market equilibrium than would be the case without law enforcement. In our diagram, this is represented by the shift in supply from SS to S'S' and the shift in demand from DD to D'D'. Market equilibrium is reduced from 0a to 0c. The market price for goods still exchanged might rise or fall, depending on the relative shifts of the supply and demand functions. In the case illustrated, supply has decreased relatively more than demand, which has raised the market price from 0b to 0d.

Society can decrease supply by increasing the costs of the suppliers. But these rises in cost must be *effective* rises, and not merely exist on paper. For example, does increasing the sentence imposed for a particular crime actually raise the criminal's costs significantly? I can't answer that one, nor can anyone else. Histori-

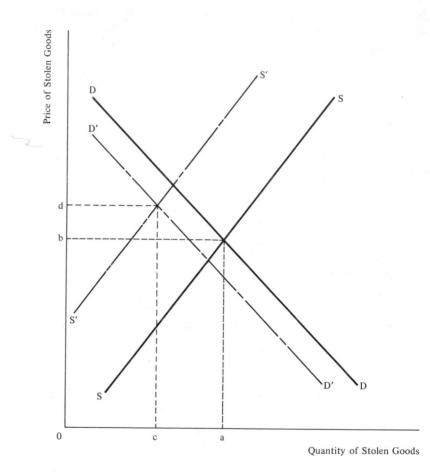

Figure 3.4 The Market for Stolen Goods

cal evidence tends to make this proposition seem somewhat doubt-ful, however. But raising the probability of getting *caught* with increased expectations of at least some punishment would undoubt-edly raise the costs. Of course, raising these expectations means that results must occur and be publicized. Generally, this means expenditure of additional resources on law enforcement.

If there were some way of *reducing* the technology available to thieves, this would help lower supply. However, there doesn't seem to be much that society can do to make this approach worth-while. Increases in technology, on the other hand, can contribute substantially to an increase in supply, as has been pointed out already.

ICP costs provide one variable about which the community can do something. For example, the impact of greater police action would be felt, since increased enforcement efforts would increase the policing costs ("antipolicing costs") of the suppliers. Substan-tial resources could also be spent trying to make the information and contracting costs of the small operator prohibitively high. And since the vast majority of stolen goods are marketed through inter-mediaries who specialize in such marketing operations, these inter-mediaries provide a bottleneck in the flow of stolen goods from suppliers to demanders; and this bottleneck provides society with a potentially efficient striking point, as we will see below.

THE ROLE OF THE FENCE

We have already made several references to the specialization that one would expect to develop in the stolen goods market. The sales intermediary is one example of it. No one really knows just how well organized the business of "fencing" stolen goods actu-ally is in this country. Nor is there any good information on the true extent of organized crime's involvement in the distribution process. It is certainly reasonable to hypothesize that fences—inde-pendent marketing specialists—handle the bulk of the transactions between thief and buyer. Because of the fairly obvious economies of scale, it is also logical to assume that fences, whether they

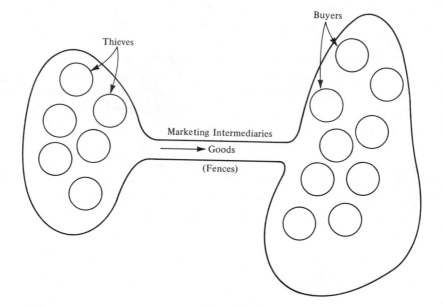

Figure 3.5 Marketing Stolen Goods

are part of a nationwide network or not, will represent many sellers and many buyers at the same time. This is no different than the wholesalers and retailers of legal goods. In Figure 3.5, this bottleneck effect of marketing intermediaries is illustrated. Many producers (in this case, the thieves) sell their products through a single fence, who in turn sells to many buyers. Often this process may consist of several stages. Some fences may operate primarily as wholesalers and distributors, while others engage in broader retail type operations.

In passing, it should be noted that there is another strong incentive for a multistage distribution process. The criticism is often leveled at big operations (big business, big labor unions, big government) that size and bureaucracy depersonalize the function being carried out. In this instance, such a depersonalization is a real plus. The less one stage knows about the operations of the other stages, the safer everyone is throughout the system. But multistaged or not, there is almost certainly a degree of activity concentration in the marketing intermediary's operation which is not found among the thieves or the demanders of hot merchandise.

The potential importance of this hypothesis is its implications for crime control. The problem of nailing tens, hundreds, thousands, or hundreds of thousands of potential stolen goods buyers is enormous. Stopping thefts is also a problem of overwhelming proportions, given existing incentives. But attacking the middlemen can work simultaneously to *reduce demand* and *reduce supply* as well. It is really a case of reversing the normal approach of trying to improve the efficiency and lower the ICP costs of a market. In this case, we're trying to make ICP costs just as high as possible for both buyers and sellers. The fact that there are smaller *numbers* of operators involved in the transactions portion of the market gives a clue as to the most desirable attack point. Remember, most people (though clearly not all) commit property crimes because they can make money doing it. In fact, they can do better in this occupation than the other alternatives that are known to and desired by them. Making the marketing of stolen goods more expensive is a double-edged sword that reduces supply *and* demand at the same time.

MONEY AS A STOLEN GOOD

Most of the discussion thus far has been aimed at the stealing of goods other than "money." It would seem that there would be a tremendous incentive to steal money rather than other goods which must be sold before any gain can be realized. The advantage is more imagined than actual, however. Again, according to the FBI *Uniform Crime Reports,* the theft of money accounted for about 10 percent of all thefts in 1970. Why isn't this percentage larger if the whole problem of middlemen and illegal markets could be bypassed in getting rid of stolen money?

The answer is severalfold. First of all, since money *is* prized as an object of theft, most people go to much greater extremes to protect cash than they do to protect most other property. This is certainly true of large sums of cash. These extra precautions automatically raise the cost in terms of risk to any potential thief, both in an absolute sense and also relative to the theft of nonmoney property. Of course, comparatively small sums are often kept with a minimum of security by business establishments and individuals. But, in these cases, the general smallness of the take raises the expected costs to expected benefits ratio so that, again, the relative advantage of stolen *cash* is reduced.

The theft of large sums of cash raises another problem for the thief. Very often, large sums of money are accounted for in financial institutions by their serial numbers. In this case, the homogenous product, money, is no longer homogeneous. It is possible to identify *specific* bills, and this opens the possibility of tracing and identifying the culprits.

There are several alternatives open to illegal money suppliers. The first of these is to operate through a fence in the same way that they would with any other stolen goods. The fence can then share the risk and costs of distribution for a percentage of the money's face value. But, generally, to reduce the risk of spending identifiable currency, the currency must be held for long periods of time until the "heat is off." This raises another cost in getting value from the stolen property—the cost of *time*. By having to wait for the sale of the hot money, an interest or discount charge is incurred—either explicitly through the fence's charges or implicitly in forgone purchases. The time lapse also means that the risk of exposure is extended over a longer period, although the original reason for the waiting is to reduce total risk.

> BESAG: It should be pointed out that this is true only for the illegal thief; it does not include white collar thieves, cost overruns thieves, financier thieves, or the wizardry thievery of high interest rates, second mortgages, etc. If the illegal thieves realized the money to be made in legal thievery, and had the initial capital or could steal, it they might become honest citizens.

There have been some interesting reactions to increased theft rates in certain metropolitan operations. For example, many bus companies refuse to make change for their customers. Either exact change or tokens are the only things accepted, and even this currency falls directly into a safelike container which the driver is unable to open.

Increased use of credit cards reduces the amount of cash in the tills of retail establishments. To the extent that this takes place, the incentive to steal cash from these establishments is reduced. With the possibility of "all credit" transactions in the future, the opportunities for money thieves will be further reduced—particularly those of the small operator who concentrates on retail store robberies.

The use of credit cards, however, has introduced a brand new type of property crime—the stealing of cards with which fraudulent purchases can be made. Recent legislation now limits the liability of legitimate card holders to $50.00 in the event that their cards are stolen and they do not report the loss. This limitation of liability may be fine for the holder, but in some ways it is providing a bonanza for credit card thieves. The limit of liability removes some incentive for the holder of a lost card to report the loss so that the card can be canceled and stores notified. At the same time, the penalties for fraudulent use of credit cards are generally smaller than for many other types of property crimes. Here we have a situation in which the cost/benefit ratio as viewed by the criminal is quite favorable, and the expected result is taking place—the ripoff and use of as many credit cards as possible!

CHAPTER 4

Crimes Without Victims

EVERYTHING discussed thus far has involved actions on the part of a perpetrator that resulted in direct costs to a victim. A crime of violence involves costs in the form of bodily and/or psychological injury to the victim. A crime against property involves material and also perhaps psychological losses to the victim.

Now we will spend some time discussing slightly different types of acts which society's laws define as illegal. Lately these acts have been categorized as "crimes without victims," although in a strict sense this description is inaccurate. But the "victims" in these cases are people who knowingly took a course of action with knowledge and forethought (like a gambler who loses or a dope user who became a public charge through physical or mental deterioration). They have committed acts which may have imposed costs on themselves; and, indirectly, these costs may be transferred to others.

There is another group of the citizenry who might be considered "victims" of crimes against the "public morality." Those who view the use of drugs, any sex outside of the puritan position on the marriage bed, or gambling in games of chance as sinful or morally wrong suffer some psychological cost when the acts are committed. To this extent, they are indirect victims of the "immoral" act. But whether or not the law should be used to enforce a particular view of morality becomes a highly charged emotional issue to which there is no answer based on any universally accepted truth. Many people (of which the author is one) hold that individuals should be able to control their own lives and destinies without interference from the society as long as physical or material damage to *others* is not involved. Some of us even go to the point of willingly supporting persons whose decisions have led them to physical or mental disabilities. But the main point remains. These are value judgments based on personal beliefs of what constitutes right and wrong.

Nevertheless, it is possible to point out to the righteous set some of the *analytical* implications of their imposed morality. This is the primary purpose of this chapter. Although there are many similarities between all of the crimes in this category, they will be split into the drug scene, sex, and gambling.

DRUGS

Most of us imperfect humans end up taking something into our bodies for the purpose of stimulating, relaxing, relieving pain, bringing on euphoria, staying awake, or going to sleep. In reasonable quantities, these substances can be virtually harmless to most people. But some substances are extremely unpredictable in their impact on the human body and mind. Hallucinogens such as LSD (acid) or strong opiates like heroin have differing effects on different people under different circumstances. Cigarettes and alcohol also affect individuals in different ways, although heavy and prolonged use of either of these drugs is a sure way to die. For simplification, the term drugs will be used to refer to everything mentioned in this section.

Our analysis is going to revolve around two specific drugs —marijuana and heroin. The first of these, pot, is physiologically nonaddictive. While tests are currently being carried out, there is no evidence that its effects are any worse on human beings than either alcohol or tobacco. In the United States of America, its use, possession, production, or sale is prohibited by both federal and state statutes. Penalties for breaking these laws range from a figurative slap on the wrists to virtual lifetime imprisonment. While hard facts are impossible to come by, it appears that the

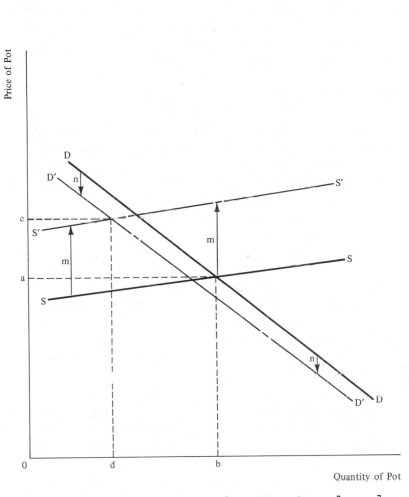

Figure 4.1 The Market for Pot-Legal and
        Illegal

basic production and marketing structure of the pot industry is close to the economist's ideal of perfect competition. There are many producers and many buyers, with little power concentration at either end of the chain. Of course, the fact that pot is illegal opens the door for "excess profits" or economic rents to be made, as we will see below.

THE POT MARKET

To begin our discussion of the pot market, imagine a situation in which the whole pot bit is legal and above board. From the law of demand, one would expect a downward sloping demand curve, such as DD in Figure 4.1. The lower the price of purchasing *and using* pot, the larger the quantity of pot demanded. For true "potheads," changes in the price would have comparatively little effect on the quantity demanded. Their demand for the product would be relatively inelastic. For others, however, there are substitutes such as booze, and to a much lesser degree, tobacco. For this group, the demand would be much more elastic.

On the supply side, there is certainly no reason to expect an unusual shape in the supply curve. Small quantities can and will be produced by resources having very low opportunity costs; therefore, some production will take place at low market prices. However, to stimulate significant increases in output, a higher market price will be required. Increased production can be obtained only by using resources that have higher opportunity costs. The supply curve will slope slightly upward to the right as with SS in Figure 4.1. There will be an equilibrium quantity marketed of 0b at a per unit price of 0a.

Now assume that the government makes pot illegal. It is now against the law to buy, sell, produce, or use pot. On the supply side, the primary impact is to raise substantially the ICP costs of suppliers. The risk involved in production and distribution has shifted the supply curve back (up) by an amount equal to *m* dollars per unit. For any given quantity, a price of *m* dollars per unit *more* will be required by suppliers.

On the demand side, the illegal nature of the good has some

effect on people's taste for the good. In general, this will lower the price people will be willing and able to pay for any given quantity of the product. Also, the risk of getting caught as a user will have an impact on tastes as well. It is also possible that the illegal nature of the good will *increase* some people's demand; but presumably this group will be small.

In any case, the net effect is that shown in Figure 4.1. Demand is reduced from DD to D'D'. Supply is reduced from SS to S'S'. The market quantity is *not* eliminated, but is reduced from 0b to 0d. Since we have assumed a greater impact on supply than on demand, the new market price is considerably higher than before—0c instead of 0a.

> BESAG: The degree of enforcement also affects the price. Two or three years ago, there was a major crackdown on marijuana. For a while the price went up, because the pot from Mexico was being cut off. But it soon went down again with new sources from Vietnam as well as some home-grown stuff. The government soon found that the cost of policing the Mexican border was prohibitive, and the resources used for that purpose could not be spent in controlling other sources. As a result of government policy, the Vietnam and home-grown pot have now established good footholds in the market. In brief, the whole project was dropped and pot was again available at the old price.

Notice that one of the arguments advanced by the antipot crowd is reinforced by the analysis thus far. Our old friend the law of demand *does* predict that legalizing pot will increase its use. But the analysis also implies another item that is often forgotten until tax time rolls around. In our example, the supply curve didn't shift because the government passed a law to make pot illegal. The supply curve shifted because resources were being used by the government to *enforce* that law. *Making* a law doesn't require many resources with high alternative costs (legislators aren't all that valuable outside of politics). But *enforcing* a law, particularly a law that many people thing is wrong, can be a very expensive proposition. This point is both important and very common with regard to *all* laws. The problems and costs of enforcement will vary inversely with the population's desire for the law itself.

In Figure 4.2, we have cleaned up the original diagram by considering only the supply and demand conditions after pot was made illegal. Increases in costs imposed by making the stuff illegal amount to ce (*m* in Figure 4.1). The old supply curve SS represents the production and marketing costs under legal conditions. This "margin" between the regular production and marketing costs and the new costs provides the incentive for our illegal supplier. This is his return for taking the chance of getting caught. This margin (ce) times the quantity sold in the illegal market (Od) produces the total revenue for the risk taker as shown by the shaded area in the figure. This is an old-fashioned "black market profit," but the word "profit" is really misused. The revenue is actually a return for taking risks and carrying out the distribution function under high cost conditions.

> BESAG: The margin of profit for pot is really not high enough for big crime to get involved. For one thing you use the raw material without much processing; therefore, the danger involved in production is low and almost anyone can produce it. More importantly, because pot is not addictive, it is difficult to develop a strong and constant clientele. For this reason, legalizing pot would not adversely affect profits for organized crime as might be the case with heroin.

THE HEROIN MARKET

We are going to make some assumptions about the heroin market that are probably realistic but hard to prove. We will also make some assumptions about the drug itself that are fairly well documented. We will assume that heroin is highly addictive in a physiological sense as well as a psychological one. Later, we

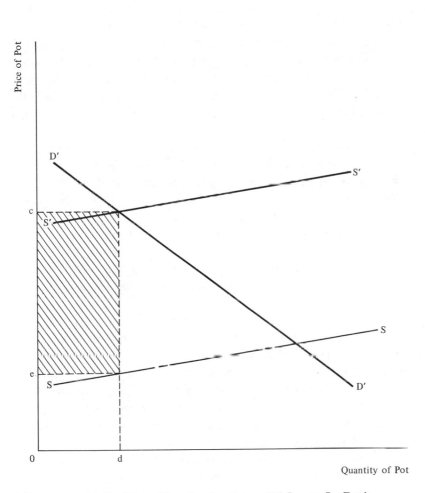

Figure 4.2 The Market for Illegal Pot

will also assume that, for most people, maintenance doses sufficient to prevent withdrawal symptoms can be taken without critical physical disabling. As to the market, the assumption will be that it is tightly controlled by a group of cooperating monopolies or a cartel; and that as far as the wholesale operation in this country is concerned, an effective monopoly exists over distribution. The entrance of monopoly into the crime scene makes for some interesting complications, particularly for those of you who have not had a full treatment of economic principles. We'll attack the problem in steps and see if the analysis can be kept to a reasonably simple level.

As a first step, we will start from a competitive model and build our more complicated monopoly model. Figure 4.3 begins with the simpleminded supply and demand curves for heroin in a competitive and legal market (MC = S and DD). The supply curve shows the *increases* in market price needed to get resources sufficient to *increase* production by additional units. In economic parlance, it is the sum of the marginal costs of all of the firms in the industry at various levels of industry output. (This assumes no secondary price effects in the markets for the employed factors of production.)

On the demand side, the demand curve (DD) shows the *average revenue* that firms in the industry will receive for various levels of output. Unlike the supply curve, the demand function shows *average* prices for *all* output produced at potential industry output levels. Remember, the supply curve shows *marginal costs* that the industry will face if production is increased. Since the industry is (by assumption) competitive, this competition will force output up to the point where the cost of producing an additional unit will exactly equal the price received by firms for the product. Profits over and above the minimums required to keep the factors (including management and capital owners) producing in this employment are competed away.

The demand curves viewed by each of the competitive firms are completely elastic. At the market price, each of the firms could sell all they could economically produce. No one firm is strong enough to have any appreciable impact on the price of the product

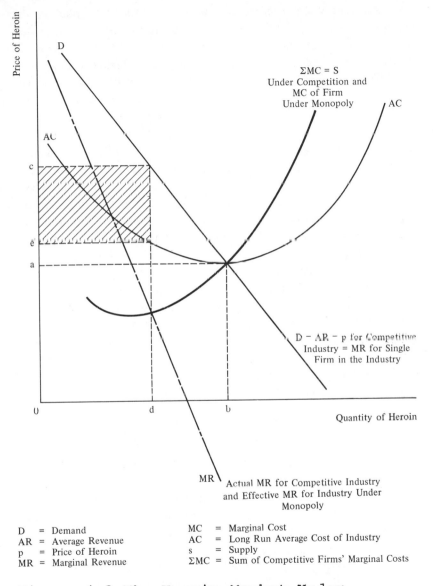

Figure 4.3 The Heroin Market Under
         Competition and Monopoly

D = Demand
AR = Average Revenue
p = Price of Heroin
MR = Marginal Revenue

MC = Marginal Cost
AC = Long Run Average Cost of Industry
s = Supply
ΣMC = Sum of Competitive Firms' Marginal Costs

by changing its own output. For this reason, the *marginal revenue* (revenue received for additional units of output) is equal to the *average revenue* for *each of the firms*. Since this is true, the industry *acts as though* its demand curve (average revenue curve) was the same as its marginal revenue curve (DD = MR in Figure 4.3).

This fact leads us to the more familiar proposition that the long-run equilibrium output of this industry and its firms will be that level at which the revenue received from producing one more unit will exactly equal the additional cost of producing that unit. Production will take place at the level where *marginal cost* and *marginal revenue* are equal. In Figure 4.3, this level is illustrated by Ob, and the market price is 0a. At this level, not only do marginal cost and marginal revenue equal each other, but *average revenue* and *average cost* also equal each other. From this last point comes the (hopefully) familiar fact that a truly competitive market will produce a situation in which the resources paid for a product will exactly equal the minimum amounts needed to produce the good. All resources received are paid out by firms in the industry to the factors of production. And more important, the amounts paid are the *minimum* amounts needed to keep the factors producing in their current occupation. From this whole set of propositions comes the idea that competitive markets are an efficient way to allocate the scarce resources used in the production and distribution of goods and services.

> BESAG: All of this holds true for legal drugs as well. Generic drugs and home remedies which can be manufactured by any producer tend to fall under the rubric of competitive drugs, and are far cheaper. However, patented trade name drugs are monopolies of the single manufacturer who holds the patent. These drugs are expensive, the demand is usually high, and the production is kept somewhat low. For example, in Korea, it was cheaper to buy penicillin on the competitive black market than it was in the monopolistic pharmacy houses.

Now let's see what happens when this competitive market

is taken over by a single firm, thereby creating a *monopoly*. The monopoly will be maintained by restricting any other firm's entry into the industry. In the analysis that follows, a crucial assumption is made—i.e., that the *cost* structure facing the new monopoly will be just the same as the cost structure facing the previously competitive industry. Of course, the fact that there is now a single seller of the product need not have any direct effect on demand; indeed, we will assume that the change does not influence demanders' desires for the product. Under these assumptions, DD, AC, and MC all stay the same.

Now comes the part that may be difficult for many of you who have not had a full-blown principles course. The demand curve shows that average revenue (price) is falling as increased quantities are made available. This is the law of demand. It tells us that if one more unit is to be sold, the price of *all* units must fall. Thus, the *revenue gained* by the firm from selling one more unit is less than the money received for that specific unit. It equals the money received from the sale of the last unit *minus* the revenue lost from lowering the price of all other units sold. *Marginal revenue* must be *less* than average revenue for all levels of output. What does this mean for output and price in the monopolized industry?

Like any other firm (including competitive firms), the monopoly will try to operate at an output level where the revenue derived from an additional unit of production will just equal the cost of producing that additional unit. It, too, will try to operate where marginal cost and marginal revenue are equal. If it produces less than this output, then increased output will bring in revenues that are greater than costs. If it produces an output greater than the optimal, production costs will exceed the revenues derived from the sale of the additonal output. Total *profit* will be less in both cases as compared to the output level at which MR = MC.

The critical difference between the actions of our monopoly as compared to those of the many firms in the competitive example lies in the fact that the monopoly *can control the total output of the industry*. Remember, by definition, the monopoly *is* the industry and can adjust its output levels as it sees fit. Again referring back to Figure 4.3, competitive output would be at level 0b. When the industry becomes monopolized, its *effective* marginal revenuecurve shifts from DD back and down to MR. Given our assumption of similar cost conditions, the level of output at which marginal cost and marginal revenue are now equal is 0d. 0d (the monopoly output level) will always be less than 0b (the competitive output level) *given the same cost functions for the monopolistic and competitive alternatives.*

If output will be reduced under monopoly, what then will happen to the market price of the product? As long as the law of demand holds, price will go up. It is precisely this potential price rise that gave the firm the incentive to lower output in the first place. It is *not* that they are trying to get the "highest" price possible for their product, nor are they trying to produce at the "cheapest" per unit cost. The monopolist, *like any other firm,* tries to maximize profit—the difference between total revenue and total cost. In the absence of competition, the monopolist can raise price and still sell his product since entry into the industry can't take place. But he will only raise price enough to bring about the profit-maximizing level of production, where the cost of producing one more unit equals the revenue received from the sale of that unit.

At output 0d, we can see the other impact of monopoly operation. The *average cost* of producing each unit at that output level equals 0e. But this level of output can be sold for an average revenue (price) of 0c. There is an average difference between receipts and costs equal to ec. This difference per unit times the number of units (0d) produces the area shown by shading in Figure 4.3; it represents the excess profit, monopoly profit, or economic rent received by the monopolist. This is the difference between the value of resources received by the monopolist for his product and the value of the resources paid out to the factors of production for his output. It is also the value of resources paid for the product *over and above* the minimum required by those resources to produce at this level.

Let's stop for a moment and see what all this means when applied to the heroin market. Remember, we are assuming rightly or wrongly that the production and distribution of heroin is a virtual monopoly. If this is the case, maybe society should bless and support the good old mob since its monopolistic organization probably tends to reduce output and increase the market price of the illegal product. This would be an interesting hypothesis indeed! Why not encourage all criminal activity to be centralized through a single controlling firm which would then act to maximize its monopoly profits by raising price and reducing output? Sure, they will make a monopoly profit; but this may turn out to be less than the value of resources that would otherwise be spent on policing activities to accomplish a comparable output reduction. The monopoly might be able to do a cheaper, more effective job of limiting entry into the field than could the police. We might even grant their illegal activities immunity from prosecution as far as reports delivered to the Internal Revenue Service were concerned. In this case, we could tax their operations, and society could cash in on a portion of their excess profits.

What *economic* reason is there against such a course of action? The most probable answer to this question is contained in the following hypothesis. As organized crime gets bigger in its scale of operations, the cost function of the organization does *not* stay the same, as assumed in the analysis above. On the contrary, there are many reasons to believe that substantial economies of scale exist in this industry. In other words, as the scale of operations increases, the *average* cost of doing business decreases. Be careful! *Total cost* continues to increase, but at a decreasing rate. This means that a monopolized industry might in fact produce a *larger* output at a *lower* price than would be the case under competitive conditions.

In Figure 4.4, this possibility is illustrated. The long-run average cost curve for the industry is shown by LAC. At output levels of less than Oa, the average cost of producing heroin exceeds the average revenue received from the sale of it. If this scale of operation could be maintained, we would have our "perfect law," where the lowest price at which suppliers are willing to produce is greater than the maximum price buyers are willing and able to pay. The average cost curve of the firm or firms operating in

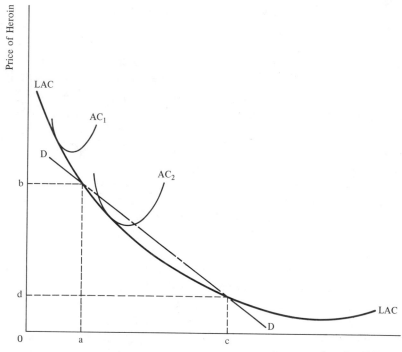

Figure 4.4 The Heroin Market with
         Economics of Scale

this range is illustrated by AC_1. But as output increases, the *average* cost of production decreases. This implies that a larger firm can produce cheaper [per unit] than a smaller firm, and thus there is a tendency for firms to get larger and larger. In the range of output between Oa and Oc, the firm or firms in the market can make a profit. Average revenue exceeds average costs. But the largest firm will make the largest profit, and can increase this profit even more by getting larger still. Thus there will be a strong tendency for the little guys to be swallowed up by the big guys, until there is only one big guy left. This single firm might have an average cost curve similar to AC_2.

We've left out the marginal curves, but if you check you will find that they fit just fine in the analysis. And, again, actual outputs will take place at the level at which marginal cost equals marginal revenue. Is it reasonable to expect that the costs facing the producer/distributor of heroin actually look like this? The answer is yes for the following reasons. The number of sources of the raw material (opium) are relatively limited. This means that policing is comparatively easy, which makes illegal distribution much more difficult than it is in the case of pot where sources of supply might be as close as a neighborhood pasture. Clearly, there is going to be a crying need for police payoffs and protection against the various agencies involved in the anti-heroin industry. But small scale competitive operations might not produce the volume needed to support such a service organization. Put another way, the development of a large-scale operation could make it possible to utilize economically a full-scale protection system as well as an international manufacturing and distribution chain. The acknowledged existence of large-scale organized syndicates operating cooperatively but with generally well defined and nonoverlapping territories and interests lends support to the hypothesis that we are indeed dealing with a *decreasing cost* industry. As the scale of operations increases, the average cost of doing business decreases.

Going back to an earlier point, it is true that the monopoly's output will be less and prices higher than would be the case if the industry were competitive *with the same cost function*. But the whole point is that costs were *not* the same for the monopolist.

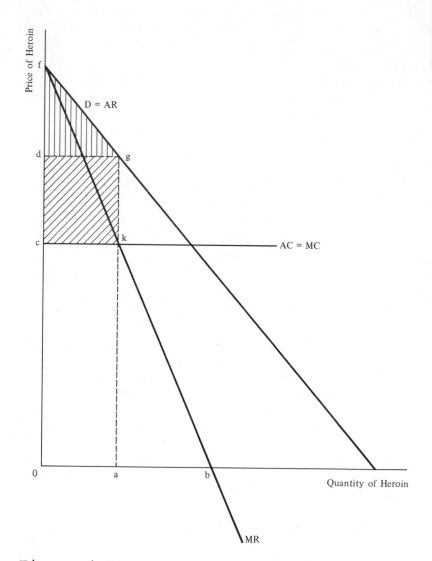

Figure 4.5 A Pusher's Market for Heroin

He is able to operate with much lower average costs than could the competitive firm. Therefore, the effect of monopoly is not to reduce output and increase the price of heroin; on the contrary, it serves to raise output and lower price. In fact, the existence of the monopoly may be the only reason that profits can be made in this endeavor, given the resources society spends opposing it.

Yet another interesting characteristic of the heroin market comes about because of the monopolistic distribution system *and* the fact that heroin is strongly addictive. On the retail end of the chain, the friendly dope pushers generally know their individual customers quite well. Some develop lifetime associations with their clients, starting with free samples in the junior high playground and ending with the ultimate bummer from an overdose. This intimate knowledge of the degree to which each of their customers is hooked can be—and is—parlayed into a beautiful example of what economists call a *discriminating monopolist*. It works out to be a supplier's dream and a demander's nightmare.

In Figure 4.5, we have shown the market situation facing a pusher at the retail level. One slightly different assumption is made in this case about the costs of the firm—the pusher. Here we assume that his costs are constant. This does *not* mean that it costs him the same total regardless of output, but rather that his costs remain proportional to output. Selling one more unit costs him the same amount as selling the previous unit. The marginal costs equal the average costs for all outputs in the range we're interested in. Now start with the proposition that the pusher is able to sell *each* customer a fix at the highest price each customer is willing and able to pay. Thus, the most addicted client will pay a price of 0f. The next one will pay slightly less, and the following one even less. Finally, the last person still in the market will just barely pay 0d which is the minimum price our pusher will accept. In other words, by knowing the degree of addiction of each of his clients, the pusher is able to get all of the so-called consumers' surplus out of the market. The area dfg now represents the *additional* profits the pusher gained by charging each customer a different price. Already, he is able to get monopoly rent in the amount of dgkc by restricting output to the point where marginal revenues

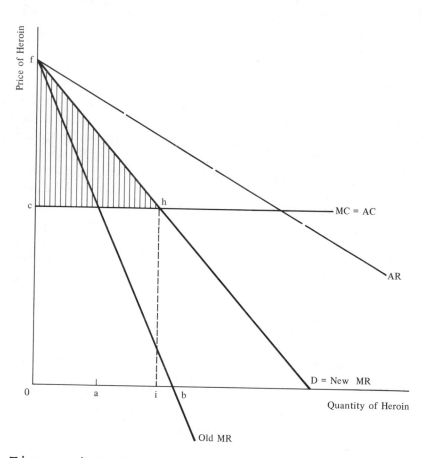

Figure 4.6 The Pusher's Market for Heroin
           with Complete Price Discrimination

and costs are equal. Now, he is adding to the pot by taking the discrimination profits as well.

Some of you have probably figured out that something else must take place before our friendly peddler can actually pull off this neat trick with success. What's to prevent a customer who is only willing to pay an amount less than the maximum (0f) from buying at the cheaper price and then reselling to the most addicted customer? This way the new middleman could pick up part of the discrimination profits for himself.

From our limited knowledge of the true mechanics of the dope operation, one big answer comes through. In general, the retail markets seem to be organized around specific territories and/or customers. There is little or no competition between pushers. In fact, if one pusher invades the territory or takes customers from another pusher, he may find himself in a ditch with some extra holes in his body. The wholesalers tend to back up and enforce the monopoly positions (including the discriminatory advantages) of the retailers. And well they should! You can be sure that a portion of these excess rents end up in the pockets of the parent firm.

There is another point that needs to be made in our analysis. All along we have been saying that any firm, competitive or monopolistic, will try to operate at the output level where marginal costs and marginal revenues are equal. We have also noted that the marginal revenue for a monopoly is always less than the average revenue (or less than demand). With a *discriminating* monopolist, however, this is no longer true. If he is able to capture the *maximum* each customer is willing and able to pay, then the demand curve (average revenue without discrimination) becomes the marginal revenue curve. This is illustrated in Figure 4.6. Note that MR in Figure 4.5 has shifted out to D in Figure 4.6. Now marginal revenue and marginal cost are equal at output 0i (greater than 0a). The consumers' surplus captured by the price-discriminating pusher goes up from dgf to chf. The net effect on output is to raise it well beyond that which would occur in a simple nondiscriminating monopoly. Keep in mind that there are two necessary conditions for price discrimination to take place. Some

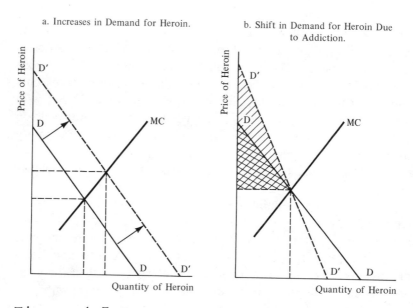

a. Increases in Demand for Heroin.

b. Shift in Demand for Heroin Due to Addiction.

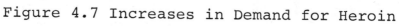

Figure 4.7 Increases in Demand for Heroin

kind of "addiction" must be present for this good (the demand curve must slope downward), and the discriminator must be able to prevent resale of the product by nonuser customers.

What are the implications of all this? First of all, the illegality of drugs provides an opportunity for risk and distribution profits for those that continue to do business in the illegal good. A nonaddictive drug such as pot does not provide the supplier with as much profit as an addictive drug. In the latter case, addiction increases the potential consumer surplus which the supplier can capture *if* he attains a monopolistic position in the market he serves. In addition, economies of scale also tend to develop a monopolistic structure in hard drug supply. Since the traffic is already illegal, there is no way the public can be protected from discriminatory practices in pricing; and this fact increases the incentive for the organized mob.

One of the most appalling characteristics of a well organized marketing organization for illegal heroin is its incentive structure to hook additional customers. In the words of singer Tom Lehrer, "They give away free samples because they know full well, today's young innocent faces are tomorrow's clientele." You said it all, Professor Lehrer! From the pusher's standpoint, the younger he can get them hooked, the longer he will have a customer and the *quicker* he can obtain a really high-paying addict. As long as society insists on making heroin illegal and heroin users criminals, these incentives will remain; and we will continue to shake our heads in wonderment at the effective sales organization of the dope pushers and their suppliers.

Before leaving the subject of addiction, there is one last point to cover. A good dope pusher is constantly trying to expand his profit just like any other businessman. If he can increase the demand for his product, this will certainly help. In other words, he tries to shift the demand curve facing him outward to the right as in Figure 4.7a. Thus far we have assumed that the pusher's supply function was completely elastic. Increases in his business did not raise the per unit cost of doing business. But this assumption may be wrong. Increases in the demand he faces and the resulting increase in business may raise the probability of his detection and capture. I suspect that the risk of his being ratted on by the "less hooked" portion of his clientele is also greater.

But addiction promotes another kind of shift in demand. Addiction *means* that the quantity demanded of the good becomes less responsive to changes in price. This is shown as a rotation shift in Figure 4.7b. What a wonderful world for the pusher! The total amount marketed hasn't increased, but the amount of surplus which the price discriminator is able to capture *has* increased.

What would happen if heroin were suddenly made legal? Obviously, the inital impact of such legalization would be to increase the equilibrium quantity marketed. Since most of the current expense in heroin can be attributed to illegal distribution costs, it is almost certain that legalization would reduce the supply price of the drug. Undoubtedly, this would cause some increase in quantity demanded; the degree of that increase would depend upon the elasticity of demand. This is an interesting point, because true addicts would probably not have their quantity demanded increase appreciably. Of course, potential new customers might now be more readily enticed to try the drug. And, on balance, the opponents of legalized hard drugs are probably correct in asserting that usage would increase.

Several other probable effects could also be expected. For example, the tremendous incentive to hook the very young by offering samples of the product would automatically be eliminated—not reduced, *eliminated*. As with all opiates, heroin is a comparatively cheap substance to produce and market *legally*. It is the present illegal nature of the beast that produces the fantastically high prices and widely variant quality. If this potential for large profit margins were eliminated by making the product available through legal channels, all incentive to hook newcomers would be removed. My guess (and a lot of other people's as well) is that the long-run effect of legalization would be to *reduce* the quantity demanded, due to the lack of merchandising of the legal product. Perhaps the legalization should take the form of availability only under medical supervision. As long as this supervision was readily available to any potential addict, the same purpose would be served.

Certain drugs, such as the opiates, have had a moral issue develop about their use. Many believe it is *morally wrong* to depend on some addictive substance for survival or a "happy" life. There is no problem with people holding such moral convictions. As a matter fact, I rather share this view of using opiates. But this is an entirely different issue than that of making the use of opiates *illegal*. It is this latter step that causes all the problems. If society really wants to get rid of dope usage, let society (which means each of us individually as well as collectively) address itself to the solution of the *causes* of dope usage. The school child being conned by a pusher is one thing, but the more common reason for dope usage has to do with the basic economic and social problems that most societies face today. Unless the problems of hopelessness, lack of opportunity, injustice, and oppression (real or imagined) are addressed, the basic reason for the dope traffic will remain. As is so often the case, in the matter of hard drugs we fight the outward and visible sign of the problem; this gives us an effective smoke screen to hide the root causes, which we refuse to face.

THE ALCOHOL MARKET

Basically, the use of the drug alcohol is legal. True, there are communities which continue to carry on the disastrous experiment of prohibition; but they are small in number and in area. A few paragraphs about this drug and its recent legal history are very much in order at this point.

For many people (some estimates run as high as 9 million in the U.S.), alcohol is a serious problem. They develop a dependency, and their constant excessive use usually causes physiological problems. On the other hand, many more millions of U. S. citizens use alcohol as a comparatively harmless depressant which interferes very little with their productive lives in the community.

Some people view the use of alcohol in precisely the same light as others view the use of heroin. It is a sin, damned by God and destructive to man. For a brief period in our history, this group succeeded in imposing their morals on the entire country. We had prohibition. Lots of great development programs took place during this period. Organized crime went through the greatest development period in its history. Never was there such a broadly based demand for an illegal product. Good old-fashioned American ingenuity really worked overtime to devise ways and means of subverting the law and screwing the Feds. Lots of people went blind and others died because of the substitutes that often found their way into the illegal distribution channels.

Finally, the country dumped prohibition. Did this eliminate the problems of alcoholism? Certainly not. Drinking—including *problem* drinking—has increased no matter how you read the numbers. But a gut blow was dealt to a whole range of other illegal activities when the profits of prohibition were denied to organized criminal forces. Had gambling, prostitution, and dope also been legalized at the same time, we would probably have been reading about Al Capone as the last of the mobsters instead of one of the founding fathers of today's crime empire.

The point I am trying to make is simply this: when *anything* that anyone wants (and is willing to pay for) is made illegal, there will be some incentive to establish an illegal market in that commodity. When this illegal good or service involves substantial costs to others, the law must step in and society must weigh the costs and benefits of prohibition and enforcement. When the only direct victim is the perpetrator himself (or perhaps only those in his family), society must weigh the costs of imposed morality carefully. Perhaps, on balance, they will decide that it is worth having a cartel of organized criminal activity for the benefit of being able to say that certain acts are immoral *and illegal*. But whatever their judgments, they (we) cannot afford to ignore both sides of the morality cost/benefit sheet.

PROSTITUTION

While the title of this section refers to the sale of sexual services (generally the sale of a woman's services to a man), the discussion really applies to the whole range of sexual activity that certain people consider immoral and certain states consider illegal. Actually, there is nothing new in the analysis, which merely consists of using the tools we have applied to other criminal acts. Some of the specific analytical conclusions are interesting, however, and warrant the few pages that follow.

We are dealing with one of the world's oldest professions—if not the oldest. It involves a contract between two people to perform a sexual act or acts. We have some civil contracts in this country which also imply performance of such acts over relatively longer periods of time. We call these contracts "marriage." Of course, there are differences between these two contracts in terms of the responsibilities for other assorted duties assumed by both parties. Generally, the services of a prostitute will not include (intentionally) the bearing and raising of children. Also, unlike many housewives, prostitutes are not required to cook the contracting partner meals, clean his living establishment, or do any number of other domestic services to earn her fee. Generally, the contract of a prostitute involves specific services for a brief period of time. The contract can be renewed many times, but it is viewed as consisting of separate transactions rather than a continuing one. True, a full-time mistress or gigolo has a continuing contract, but this arrangement is somewhat more like the marriage situation rather than simple prostitution.

In Figure 4.8, we show a simple competitive prostitution market. By now this should be very familiar. The demand curve merely illustrates the proposition that as the price of the service falls, the quantity demanded will rise—and vice versa. The supply curve assumes that as the market price rises, the quantity of prostitution services supplied will increase. Given a free and legal market, the price will be 0b with an equilibrium quantity of 0c.

If prostitution is outlawed, the costs imposed by operating illegally will shift the supply function up (back) by an amount

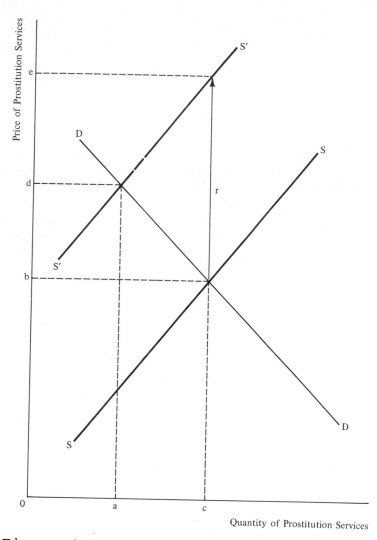

Figure 4.8 Comparing Legal and Illegal
Prostitution

equal to r. Since we are assuming (reasonably) that there is some elasticity of demand, this decrease in supply will both lower market quantity and raise market price, such as 0a and 0d respectively in Figure 4.8. Were demand completely inelastic, the price would absorb all of the adjustment and rise to 0e with no change in the market quantity.

There are some side effects that also require mention at this time. People are often concerned today about consumer protection. There is a great deal of discussion about imposing government standards and quality controls on consumer goods and services. In a legal and free market, much of this problem disappears by the action of the market itself. Say a given supplier puts out a poor quality product; if he has many competitors, he won't last long. People will shift to other suppliers who are turning out the quality desired by the marketplace. On the other hand, if the market is controlled by a supplier or cooperating group of suppliers, this automatic competitive quality control is lost or diminished in effectiveness.

This same situation takes place if a product is made illegal. The illegality of the product makes the passing of information both difficult and expensive. This is part of the total cost increase represented in Figure 4.8 by the reduced supply function. Specifically, organized enterprises such as houses of prostitution will be reduced due to the ease with which they can be identified and shut down by police. Those houses remaining in business will be operating without the degree of competition that would otherwise be the case. Information about the relative quality of one establishment versus another will not be so readily available or transmitted. In addition, many girls will probably take to the streets where detection and arrest is generally more difficult. Here again, information about the comparative quality of competing services will be harder to come by.

Why should society care about all this? Isn't a reduction in quality precisely one of the goals of making prostitution illegal? As many of you have probably surmised, "quality of product" in this case has a dimension of crucial interest to the public at large. Venereal disease in this country has been on the increase at alarming rates over the past few years. There is almost no question that most of this phenomenal increase is due to an increase in sexual intercourse among young unmarried adults. Of course, they are not necessarily involved in prostitution. But the same morality that results in making prositution illegal also results in creating reluctance on the part of VD sufferers to seek treatment.

The same sexual permissiveness mentioned above will probably have a significant impact on the market for prostitution services. It has the economic effect of making the price of a substitute good very much cheaper. This, in turn, can be expected to decrease the demand for prostitutes. The amateurs are ruining the business!

One final point should be made. Illegal prostitution still provides a source of revenue for organized crime. While the importance of this activity has undoubtedly decreased, there is evidence that the mob still has considerable interests in the profession. Not only does this add strength to organized crime, but the monopolistic structure of the mob makes possible the exploitation of the individual prostitutes.

GAMBLING

The final category of our discussion of crimes without victims is gambling. Most of the points made in the other portions of this chapter apply here as well, and they will not be repeated. Again, there are many markets in the country for various "games of chance." In some areas, these games are legalized; in others, they are treated as serious criminal activity. Organized crime gets into the act very quickly in areas where they and the local moralists have succeeded in getting laws passed to prohibit gambling. Profits from gambling rank with proceeds from hard dope as one of the biggest sources of monopoly profits for the mob.

> BESAG: There is good reason to believe that organized crime is also involved in legal gambling, particularly in Nevada. Even though the state has placed strong restric-

tions on who can own gambling establishments, it would appear that organized crime gets some of its greatest resources from the Nevada gaming tables. This might be distinguished from state lotteries, where all of the revenues go to the state directly and profits consist of a commission on the number of tickets sold. Whether organized crime is involved in state lotteries is again a moot point, since organized crime seems to be in a lot of legitimate businesses.

Gambling has its addicts. There are people who will blow their last cent on the horses, numbers game, or local floating crap game. The moralists argue (as they do in the case of hard dope) that legalizing gambling will increase this behavior. More and more people will spend their family's meager incomes on gambling instead of buying milk for the baby. There is undoubtedly some truth to this assertion, but the increase in this category of gambler is at least subject to question. If the person is truly an *addict*, this means that he will gamble with very little thought to the expected costs. His gambling will *not* be very responsive to changes in the cost of the activity. His demand for gambling will be relatively inelastic. If this is the case, then the number of compulsive gamblers may not increase with legalization. They are already doing their thing while the action is illegal.

On the other hand, there are many of us who would undoubtedly play the tables if the activity could be carried out locally. For the "casual" gambler, it is reasonable to predict that his demand for gambling is quite elastic—elastic with regard to *price* changes and increases in income. As incomes go up, one would expect the demand for this type of gambling to go up. For casual gamblers, the activity is a luxury good and has many substitutes in the form of other recreational activities. Therefore, legalization would undoubtedly increase this group's gambling operations.

But one major point for legalization should be noted in passing. If the activity is legalized and *taxed* by governmental bodies, a whole new source of revenue opens up. Basically, the government can capture a portion of the monopoly rents that are presently accruing to the mob. It's an interesting moral point all by itself. If gambling is morally wrong, why not let the rotters blow their resources, have the government collect a portion of the profits, and then buy good things for us good guys? Again, it is a choice that may not be accepted, but it cannot be ignored.

Chapter 5

Who Gains and Who Loses?

WE'RE going to continue this presentation with a brief discus
sion of the gains and losses from illegal activity. Society, the victim, and the criminal will all be considered.

Obviously, the impact on society will be quite different for
different types of crime. When a good is stolen, it doesn't just
disappear; its rightful owner no longer has it, but someone else
does. When a man is beaten in a mugging, the effects don't end
when the mugger runs off down the street. When a thief is sent
to prison for ten years, society may forget him, but the impacts
of his incarceration will continue to act upon and within the com
munity.

The analysis we will use here involves a look at the lifetime
earnings flows of the people involved. You should be careful when
interpreting these figures. From the standpoint of the individual
or individuals, a net increase in earnings can be assumed to be
a net increase in benefits. When potential earnings are forgone,
the opposite can be assumed. It would be easy to carry this
measure of private benefits into the concept of social benefits as
well. After all, if a person receives a payment for services ren-
dered, then someone must have valued the service *at least* to the
extent of the value paid. Of course, it's entirely possible that an
employee's wage may be less than the value the employer would
have been willing and able to pay on an all-or-nothing basis. The
operation of the market may result in a *consumer's surplus*
(remember, the boss is consuming the worker's product—labor.
The market may also yield a surplus for the worker—*a producer's*

surplus. In any case, a person's earnings represent the minimum value to society of his services.

If all this is true, can't we say that a reduction in potential wages also represents a lost production potential to the community? The answer is yes, but. . . . If a skilled welder capable of earning $12,000 per year is put in prison and paid $125 per year to produce license plates, the Gross National Product may well fall by $11,875 or perhaps even some multiple of that figure. But while national output has decreased, so have the payments made by society to the welders. Only if there have been external benefits not reflected in the welder's wages will there actually be a net societal loss.

There are some other minor impacts that can reflect additional losses to the community, such as the reduced taxes collected from the incarcerated worker. Also, if the imprisonment of the bread-winner of a family results in his family's requiring welfare assistance, this too will have to be counted in the loss column. Notice that there is a big problem here in going from the *micro* analysis of the individual to the *macro* analysis of the whole country. It is easy to talk about a reduction in the productivity of one individual being offset by the reduced resources paid to that individual. However, if you carry this out to cover any significant portion of the producing public, your economy will grind to a halt.

Anyway, this shows you some of the problems of interpreting the values of income streams. Clearly, the private impact can be partially measured using this technique, but the social cost/benefit impact must be approached with care and skepticism.

COST ANALYSIS OF A MURDER

Let's assume that a 22-year-old high school graduate murders a 22-year-old senior in college. If the victim has been subsidized by the community to obtain his education, then this is one investment on which society will clearly lose. Again, the degree of this loss will depend on how one wishes to view the wages the graduate would have earned had he not been killed.

Anyway, for the murderer, we will assume a potential earnings profile such as that listed in Table 5.1 under the first column labeled "income". This is a hypothetical earnings profile for our subject had he *not* committed this crime nor any other. These same numbers are graphed in Figure 5. The next income column in Table 5.1 lists his earnings with the assumption of a 20-year prison stretch, during which time he earns $125 per year. Again, this series is graphed in Figure 5. The crosshatched area in Figure 5 indicates the magnitude of the difference in *total* lifetime earnings with and without the commission of the crime. Total earnings fall from $326,500 to $150,500.

Since we are talking about value over time, these total figures overstate the case to a considerable magnitude. To obtain the *present* value of *future* earnings, the face value of the future earnings must be discounted by "the" interest rate. In this case, I have assumed a fairly substantial interest rate of 8 perent per year. When this is compounded over the earning years in the profile, the numbers in terms of present value change enormously. To arrive at a common point, all figures have been discounted back to an age of 16 years, which is assumed to be the beginning of the working lifetimes of the people involved. Thus the value of a $500 salary (we've assumed it is all received at the end of the working year) becomes $463 when discounted back to the beginning of the working year. Similarly, an $8,000 income at age 40 is reduced to a value of $1,168 at age 16. Carrying out this process for all earning years results in a total *discounted* earnings stream of $57,431 for the perpetrator had he not committed the crime, and $15,962 if he did. The discounted loss becomes $41,469, as compared to the gross loss in earnings of $176,000.

The same series of figures and calculations are now made for the victim. Assuming he had not been killed, an earnings profile such as shown in Table 5.1 could be hypothesized. This profile is graphed in Figure 5.2, along with the profile of earnings that pertained with the murder taking place. The gross earnings difference in the two situations amounts to $532,000, while the discounted value reduces this figure to $83,808.

There is one other figure that needs to be considered in even

| | Perpetrator | | | | Victim | | | |
| | Without Crime | | With Crime | | Without Crime | | With Crime | |
Age	Income	Value	Income	Value	Income	Value	Income	Value
16	500	468	500	463	500	463	500	463
17	500	429	500	429	500	429	500	429
18	500	397	500	397	500	399	500	397
19	3000	2205	3000	2205	1000	735	1000	735
20	3000	2041	3000	2042	1000	680	1000	681
21	3500	2208	3500	2206	1000	630	1000	630
22	3500	2042	125	73	1000	583	1000	584
23	4000	2161	125	68	8000	4322	0	0
24	4500	2251	125	63	8500	4252	0	0
25	5000	2316	125	58	8500	3937	0	0
26	5500	2359	125	54	9000	3860	0	0
27	6000	2383	125	50	10000	3971	0	0
28	6500	2390	125	46	11000	4045	0	0
29	7000	2383	125	43	11000	3745	0	0
30	7500	2364	125	39	12000	3783	0	0
31	8000	2335	125	36	12000	3503	0	0
32	8000	2162	125	34	13000	3514	0	0
33	8000	2002	125	31	13000	3253	0	0
34	8000	1854	125	29	14000	3244	0	0
35	8000	1716	125	27	14000	3004	0	0
36	8000	1589	125	25	14000	2781	0	0
37	8000	1472	125	23	14000	2575	0	0
38	8000	1363	125	21	14000	2384	0	0
39	8000	1262	125	20	15000	2365	0	0
40	8000	1168	125	18	15000	2190	0	0
41	8000	1082	125	17	15000	2028	0	0
42	8000	1001	3000	376	15000	1878	0	0
43	8000	927	3500	406	15000	1739	0	0
44	8000	859	4000	429	15000	1610	0	0
45	8000	795	4000	398	16000	1590	0	0
46	8000	736	4500	414	16000	1472	0	0
47	8000	682	4500	383	16000	1363	0	0
48	8000	631	5000	394	16000	1262	0	0
49	8000	584	5000	365	16000	1169	0	0
50	8000	541	6500	440	16000	1082	0	0
51	8000	501	6500	407	16000	1002	0	0
52	8000	464	7000	406	16000	928	0	0
53	8000	430	7000	376	16000	859	0	0
54	8000	398	7000	348	16000	795	0	0
55	8000	368	7000	322	16000	736	0	0
56	8000	340	7000	298	16000	682	0	0
57	8000	316	7000	276	16000	631	0	0
58	8000	292	7000	256	16000	585	0	0
59	7500	254	7000	237	16000	541	0	0
60	7000	219	7000	219	16000	501	0	0
61	6500	189	6500	189	5000	145	0	0
62	6000	161	6000	161	5000	134	0	0
63	5500	137	5500	137	5000	124	0	0
64	5000	115	5000	115	5000	115	0	0
65	4500	96	4500	96	5000	107	0	0
Totals	326500	57431	150500	15962	537500	87726	5500	3918

Table 5.1

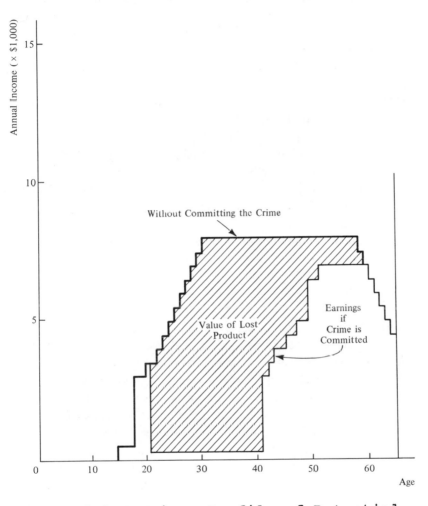

Figure 5.1 Earnings Profile of Potential
Murderer

the most elementary analysis of the cost of our crime. This is the direct cost of the incarceration of a prisoner in a maximum security institution. Figures put out by the Wisconsin State Prison at Waupun, Wisconsin, show a *direct* cost of about $4,500 per man per year. This figure does not include any allowance for capital equipment, such as buildings or other depreciable assets. It does include the main items of labor, maintenance, etc. For a 20-year term, the state would spend $90,000 to incarcerate our murderer. But to keep things in the same perspective, this figure discounted back to a comparable point to those of the income profiles would result in a discounted value of $27,841.

Now let's add up some of these figures and see what the direct cost of the murder has been:

Discounted Value of Lost Product-Victim	$ 83,808
Discounted Value of Lost Product-Murderer	41,469
Discounted Value of Direct Prison Costs	27,841
Total	$153,118

There are still a great many other costs that have not been included, such as the loss of educational resources invested in both men, the cost of the legal machinery that put the murderer in prison, and the cost of police services in maintaining law and order. But what this analysis does do is make explicit the forgone product of both victim and perpetrator. It also makes explicit the costs of incarceration, both in direct prison costs as well as in the lost product of the prisoner. This is *not* to say that no one should ever be imprisoned. It does, however, suggest that such a course of action should be carefully weighed.

COSTS OF PROPERTY CRIME

Crimes against property—that is, theft of property—raises some other issues for society. If property is stolen and then used

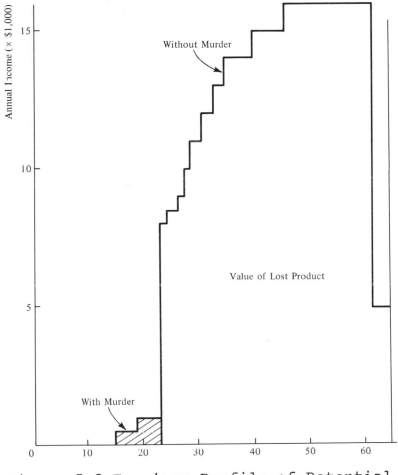

Figure 5.2 Earnings Profile of Potential
Murder Victim

by someone other than the rightful owner, the services from such property have merely been transferred. One person's loss is another person's gain. If property is simply destroyed rather than transferred, the problem is analogous to the bodily injury case in which society loses part of its product. An increase in the incidence of property crime will influence both the supply and demand for the product concerned by increasing transactions costs for demanders and suppliers. Supply will tend to be reduced, and demand will also tend to decrease.

Property crime has another impact on the resources of the community. Many people would prefer paying a known and predictable price to protect themselves against an unknown and unpredictable (to the individual) potential cost. Because of this desire, the whole business of property insurance was developed. As with any other "contingency market", property theft insurance is based on the proposition that while it is impossible to predict with certainty a theft against a specific person, it *is* possible to predict the likelihood of thefts in a larger population. If someone wishes to insure against a theft loss, he pays a premium into a pool of other insured people—a premium based on the likelihood of theft against any member of the group. If the insured then suffers a loss, the pool pays him the amount of the insured value. In this case, the individual has received back more than he paid into the pool. But if an individual does not suffer a loss, he will have paid resources in and received no material resources back. He *will* have received, however, the assurance of no risk—or at least a reduced risk—of property loss through theft.

As thefts go up, the cost of insurance against thefts will also rise. But does this represent a cost to society? Basically, the answer is no. Like this theft itself, the increase in insurance costs will represent a further crime-generated transfer of resources from some members of the contingency pool to others. Undoubtedly, the increased costs will be partially passed on to others through the usual operation of the market. However, to the extent that the extra business requires an additional expenditure of resources by the insurance companies for administration of the pool, some cost will be imposed on society by requiring resources to come into the insurance administration field out of some other alternative.

There is at least some evidence that property crime increases may take the form of "vicious circles". To some extent, such increases may well decrease the general regard for law; this, in turn, may increase enforcement problems and costs. As a result, the incidence or property crimes may go up again—and so on. We'll comment a bit more on this in the postscript.

THE MARKET FOR CRIME PREVENTION

Society does demand some measure of control over illegal activities. As has been pointed out, a *law* without enforcement (voluntary or forced) is not only ineffective but also may be destructive of other laws.

Imagine something called a "law enforcement resource unit". I haven't the faintest idea what the actual makeup of this unit might be; but it would consist of some quantity of police personnel, crime prevention programs, legal machinery, etc. It is the same kind of unit that we use in analyzing any aggregated market consisting of combinations of more than one good. For example, in macroeconomics, we talk about the supply and demand for *all output* in the economy. What one unit of this "all output" looks like is hard to imagine; nevertheless, it is useful to have these aggregate concepts.

Like suppliers of any other scarce good or resource, factors of production in the crime prevention business will make their services available at prices dependent upon their opportunity costs. Therefore, it is reasonable to assume that the supply curve for law enforcement resources will be upward sloping in the usual manner, as illustrated in Figure 5.3. In the same fashion as other markets, increases in technology will shift the supply curve to the right, while increases in costs of production will shift it to the left. Such cost increases might consist of greater money costs or increased risk of injury and death in carrying out the service.

On the demand side, we see a normal demand curve, indicating that society will be willing and able to purchase more crime

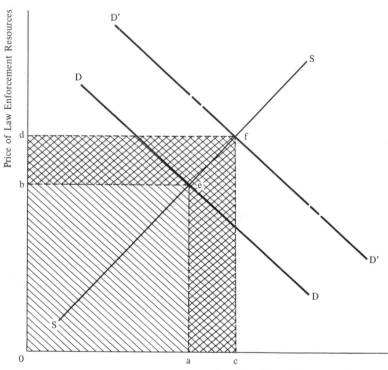

Figure 5.3 The Market for Law Enforcement
         Resources

control as the unit price of that control decreases (everything else being equal). This demand will be derived from some sort of crime control function which relates the degree of control attained for a given investment of resources. Such a control function is illustrated in Figure 5.4. It assumes decreasing marginal or additional control at high levels of control resource use, which is probably reasonable. As has been implied several times before, hitting the concentrated areas of the criminal operation would result in a large reduction of illegal activity; but trying to clean up the little guys would require staggering efforts.

> BESAG. It should be pointed out that Nixon has just announced again that they are going after the little guy. There is a plan afoot to stop heroin sales on the street by apprehending the pushers. The Nixon administration calls this "getting at the root of the problem". It is the same approach he tried when he closed the Mexican border to stop pot smoking. That move turned out to be expensive and didn't work either. Organized crime, which controls most of the heroin production, couldn't care less about the pusher on the street. He is replaceable, and the market demand from addicts is still just as great. As a matter of fact, making contacts more difficult by arresting pushers might just increase the price and make more money for the mob.

With Figure 5.4's initial crime control function C, Oa resources will result in a 50-percent control of criminal activity. To increase the level of control an additional 25 percent, additional resources will be needed—greater than the total amount required to attain the first 50 percent of control. Now let's assume that "morality" goes to hell in the society, and that many people increase their tastes for criminal activity or the fruits of such activity. In effect, this shifts the crime control function downward to C'. In this case, to attain the initial 50 percent of control will require Ob resources instead of Oa.

The chances are that such a shift will produce an increase

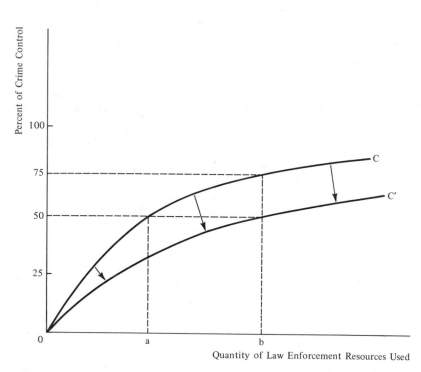

Figure 5.4 Crime Control Functions

in the demand for control resources. Obviously, this assumes that the demanders of law and order are *not* the ones whose taste for crime has increased. Were this the case, demand for law enforcement resources might actually decrease. But if a certain level of crime control is still desired and people are willing to forgo alternatives to attain it, demand will increase as in D'D' of Figure 5.3; and the total value of resources expended on crime control will rise from Obea to Odfc. This increase in value results from the increased quantity required to attain the target control level (area aefc), and also from the fact that the increased demand for control resources has raised their price (value goes up by bdfe for this reason).

BESAG: All societies change their mores, and it is usually the case that the law follows what is already accepted practice—i.e., the leaders pass laws that everyone already agrees with anyhow. The problem of late has been that with the increase in communication and mobility, more and more people who hold a minority view are finding communities where they can do what they want to. The law, however, was not made to encompass minorities within a majority. Therefore, even if the minority is sizable, laws will exist which they will break and which the conventional society will feel it has to enforce. Change is now occurring so quickly that the legislators have difficulty passing laws which are even majority positions.

In brief, a lot of people are going to be breaking the law a lot of the time, thereby increasing the cost of enforcement, etc. For example, there is a law that no one in the state of Wisconsin may buy contraceptives unless they are married. It is a stupid and unenforceable law—a joke. Sometimes some idiot tries to have the law enforced; this then makes everyone—the police, the legislators, the judge, the attornies, etc. look like idiots. It's no way to run a business.

CHAPTER 6

Some Notes on a Prison Visit

ECONOMISTS are noted for their hard hearts (or lack of heart) and their cold inhuman approach to the problems of the world. Sociologists are supposed to be good at putting the "human element" back into social science. Personally, I think both of these characterizations are ridiculous; but just so there won't be any doubt about the "human approach," I have asked Brother Besag to write a brief case history on each of three interviewees we contacted at the Wisconsin State Prison in Waupun, Wisconsin. For my part, I will attempt to stick some numbers on a *part* of the costs and benefits that society and these people have created. With this brief prologue, here's Frank!

BESAG: The state of Wisconsin has a history of building its public buildings with skill and honesty, and Waupun Prison is no exception. The prison buildings themselves are of a brownish gray sandstone, and they are separated from the outside gate by a distance of some 20 to 30 feet. The main entrance to the prison is like that of any other office building. There are no huge iron doors. There is no guard. There is no asking for permission to enter. The inside is clean, well-lit, and modern.

On the day Gus Rogers and I visited Waupun, we were immediately met by a smiling and helpful assistant warden for treatment who suggested that we chat with the warden before interviewing the prisoners. At that time, the acting warden was Elmer Cady, an urbane and humane man who has attempted to make a number of innovative and client-oriented changes in the prison. His understanding and feeling for the inmates is clear both to them and to the staff. And though there may be those who disagree with his policies, there are few who would doubt his integrity.

We talked to Warden Cady for about 20 minutes, and I presented him with a list of ten prisoners whose names I had gotten from ex-convicts and ex-staff as being men of special interest. Arrangements were made for us to interview as many inmates as we wished.

The assistant warden for treatment suggested that we take a tour of the prison while waiting for the first prisoner to be brought up. Both Gus and I were familiar with other maximum security prisons: San Quentin and Folsom in California, Attica in New York State, and a nonmaximum security prison in Arkansas. We were both expecting the worst. But to our surprise, we found that although it is obviously a prison with all of its unpleasant atmosphere, Waupun is certainly better than the others we've seen. The men are referred to by name, not number. There has obviously been an attempt to supply both training and therapy; and there is a general atmosphere of "truly this is an impossible situation; let's not make it any more impossible than absolutely necessary." The over-crowded conditions, the brutality, the general feelings of insensitivity and lack of concern which both Gus and I noticed at other prisons is not a general factor here.

This is not to imply that regimentation and insensitivity do not exist, for obviously they do. When men walk from one place to another in Waupun Prison, they walk in groups, in double file, and they pay attention only to where they are walking and how they are walking. When we said hello to inmates, they looked surprised as though they were not used to being spoken to by anyone besides staff and other inmates. Whenever we approached, prisoners would draw back and not wish to speak to each other or to us. And the staff members, if sitting at a desk, would immediately rise to their feet and greet us in what was almost a position of attention.

During our entire stay at Waupun, we saw only three inmates actually engaged in some sort of useful activity—the director of the radio programs and the editor of the newspaper and his assistant. All of the other prisoners seemed to spend most of their time standing and waiting. If we came by while an inmate was mopping the floor, he would stop mopping, draw back against the wall, and almost try to hide within it. After we left, he would remain standing by the wall and either very quietly talk to other inmates or just wait, for what we did not know, before he resumed his mopping activities.

The speech patterns of inmates, one to another, is of a peculiar quality, even in a well-run and relatively humane prison. They do not speak openly and full-mouthed as would the average person outside. Rather, when they are in view of staff and outsiders, they speak with their mouths almost closed and in a tone which makes it virtually impossible to hear what they are saying outside of the immediate group. The staff largely ignores this behavior.

In brief, everyone seems to know everyone else's name in prison. But the role interactions are so stylized that it seems difficult if not impossible for people to talk to each other except in almost a third language—the inmates speak a language to each other: the staff speak a language to each other; and when the inmates and staff communicate, they have to speak in tongues. Neither the staff nor the inmates seem to be fully three dimensional people to the other.

A separate room was made available for us at Waupun to interview the prisoners. In spite of ourselves and the good treatment that we saw around us in the prison, Gus and I could not help trying to check the room to see whether there were hidden wires and microphones. There is something about a prison which makes you distrustful and overly cautious; and although we did not find any (and I am sure there were none) microphones, there was still the feeling in the back of our minds that Big Brother was watching. In any case, the first prisoner soon came in to speak to us.

CASE HISTORY: GARY MASON

Gary Mason entered prison in 1967, at the age of 21, on a six-year sentence for writing bad checks. He spent 22 months at the Green Bay Reformatory. (Green Bay is designed for young men between the ages of 16 and 22.) In the fall of 1969, Gary left the reformatory and entered the University of Wisconsin at Green Bay as a student and computer programmer. He was an activist there, and is extremely bright and extremely concerned. But as had happened so often with Gary, he began to overspend his income; he was going out a lot and he had gotten into the use of soft drugs.

Gary told us that he intended to go back to soft drugs when he got out, but that he would never again overdraw his checking account and be revoked. The cost of being revoked had proven to be far too high. All of his "good time" was taken away, so that he had to serve the rest of his original sentence plus the "good time" that he had accumulated. (For every month that you spend in prison with no bad marks against your record, you receive a certain amount of "good time" which can be taken off your sentence by the parole board.) On the revocation, Gary spent three months at Green Bay and one year at Fox Lake.

While Gary was at Fox Lake, he began to write and was very successful at it—so successful, in fact, that he was asked to attend a Wisconsin state writers' work-shop. Because Gary had been on good behavior at Fox Lake, he was to be transferred at this time to the camp at Walworth—a minimum security situation, and sup-posedly the last station before parole and reentry into conventional society. However, Gary found out that if he went to Walworth he would have difficulty in getting released to go to the writers' workshop; the warden at Walworth evidently did not feel that he should go. Regardless of what Gary said or to whom he appealed, he was sent to Walworth two weeks before the writers' workshop; there he was told that he would not be able to attend that workshop even if someone would come by from Fox Lake and pick him up.

Two weeks later, on the night of the workshop, Gary escaped from Walworth by merely walking out of the camp. Sixteen hours later, he was caught in a "setup." An ex-convict whom Gary contacted called his own lawyer, who in turn contacted the authorities, who in turn set up a meeting where Gary could be apprehended. Gary does not blame the ex-convict, for he knows full well that parole revocation is virtually automatic if you are suspected of having helped an escaped convict. In June of 1971, Gary was sent to Waupun Prison as an escapee.

When talking about the escape, Gary said he felt that everything had come together in the "Capricorn month". The prison had come to represent to him a con-finement which was mental as well as physical. He could not send out his manuscripts for publication without their being censored and approved. A girl who had been writ-ing to him and visiting him at Fox Lake "quit him." He felt that all of the things he had been working for would come together at the writers' conference, but he was not able to go. The parole board had turned him down, and he was also turned down for school release (being able to attend an extension of the University of

Wisconsin under loose supervision). The pressures and his feeling of powerlessness to handle them became too great, and Gary walked out. A prison cannot tolerate escapes; so the full mobilization of authority, search mechanisms, and security were brought to bear on Gary Mason's escape.

When Gary talked about the effects of prison, one gained two basic impressions: the first was that, indeed, Gary has gained some very specific skills which will help him when he gets out. In particular, he is enthralled with the fact that he has learned to write. When he leaves prison, he hopes to continue his writing career on the staff of either a small town newspaper or the Milwaukee Journal. Second, and more difficult to put a name to, was the feeling one got that Gary Mason has learned to use the right words and say the right things to get himself out of prison and into a working situation. When he talked about himself in terms of the prison, he said that while he was at Green Bay he "needed to grow up," that he was "given good opportunities," and that he "worked with shrinks."

While Gary was talking, however, I felt that he was not absolutely convinced that he needed to grow up while at Green Bay, nor that therapy had really done him any good, nor that he had been really given good opportunities (with the exception of his writing). Rather I got the impression that he felt that if he was going to be paroled now from Waupun, the staff and the parole board somehow had to be convinced that he had "learned his lesson." This is obviously only my impression, and I cannot prove it; but in talking to ex-convicts, I have discovered that this certainly seems to be a method inmates use to increase their chances for parole.

(The staff members to whom I spoke privately are aware that inmates indeed do foster false impressions about what they have learned. If, for instance, Gary Mason had indicated that he would never again use soft drugs, the staff would not have believed him. It was therefore important for Gary to learn that he must maintain a balance in his fostered impressions between being unrehabilitated and being too rehabilitated.)

Gary had some impressions about the staff which were not particularly unusual but were very succinctly stated. He recognized the staff as small town people who lived 50 or 60 miles away from the nearest major metropolitan area. These staff members did not wish to think about the individual characteristics of inmates, both because they were criminals and because they came from the urban environment which the staff neither understood nor trusted. For this reason, Gary said, they tended to categorize and pigeonhole the inmates into far too tight categories. And this was his major objection to the staff.

Finally, Gary made two points which related not to what he had learned at the institution, but rather to what the institution had done and will continue to do to him. First, Gary understands fully that having been in prison (not necessarily having committed a crime, but just the act of having been in prison) will directly affect his earning power. It will be more difficult for him to get a job, and the job may be lower paying just because he has been a prisoner. However, Gary said, "People have open hearts to ex-cons"; but he also added, "I will hide it (that I'm an ex-con) if need be."

Second, and most interesting, Gary commented on prison life as a whole. He said, "In prison emotions are different—not different in degree but different in kind. No one from the outside can understand the emotions that we have." Gary didn't carry that discussion further, and we couldn't get anything more out of him about it. But a number of ex-convicts have indicated that the situation in a prison, no matter how humane, is so different from the situation outside that a series of emotional responses totally unknown to those outside become the commonplace feelings for those who are inside.

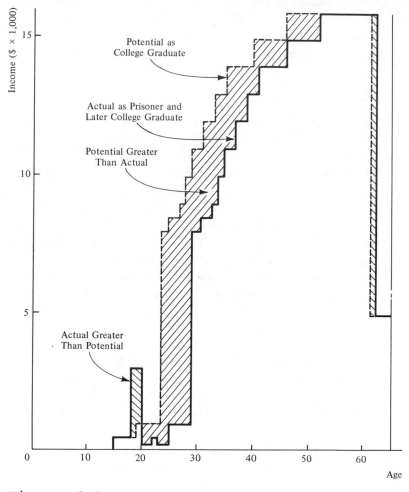

Figure 6.1 Actual and Potential Earnings
Profiles - Gary Mason

THE ECONOMIC VIEW

Gary Mason is a very bright young man. If I had to put odds on his ultimate success, they would be very high indeed. Of course, to some degree, he is a "marked man" because of his prison record. But my guess is that he may actually turn this to his advantage. In calculating an estimate of income, I have made the following assumptions about his past and future:

(1.) If he had not gotten himself in trouble with the law, he would have gone to college at the normal time. Using this assumption, his "potential" income profile in Figure 6.1 is the same as the one used earlier for a college graduate.

(2.) He will enter college and graduate within the next four years. I also assume that he will continue full-time employment a year longer than most college graduates.

(3.) His prison record will not impair his earning ability once he graduates.

Based on these assumptions the following arithmetic applies, using the discounted values demonstrated earlier:

(−) Value of Potential Earnings Without Prison	$81,173
(+) Value of Actual Earnings	55,100
(−) Value of Prison Expenses	10,581
Net Cost Valued at Age 16	$36,754

There are many pitfalls that may well change this outcome substantially. If Gary gets out soon, he will be on probation. The slightest slip can land him back in Waupun. It is probably impossible to know how much exposure to a prison a young person can take and still be able to keep the basic perspective needed to fit once more into the outside world. At some point, in spite of his brightness and rationality, Gary would probably change career plans in favor of the illegal route. As has been stated several times previously, a maximum security prison is a fine university for training in such endeavors.

The assumption that his record will not reduce his earning ability is also a strong one. He might make substantial efforts to obtain a degree only to find that no one will hire him. I doubt that this will be the case; but, given present attitudes, the possibility certainly exists.

CASE HISTORY: STEVE URBAN

Steve Urban has eyes that are absolutely blue and look right through you. But there is nothing behind them. Steve Urban is a frightening man; he has been incarcerated since October 3, 1943.

In 1943, Steve Urban got drunk one night and killed a man. That's all we know because Steve "doesn't want to talk about it." Most of the interview with Steve went the same way. He sat there staring through you, waiting for you to ask him a question; then he answered it quickly and concisely with no embellishment.

Question: "What's the difference between prison now and prison in 1943?"

Answer: "Don't beat them up no more. We get more money and better eats now."

"How long have you been here at Waupun?"

"This time?"

"Yes."

"Three years, five months."

"Where were you before?"

"Central State Hospital, for 25 years."

"What was Central State Hospital like?"

"You mind own business there. They said I was crazy."

"You don't think so though, do you?

"No."

"What did you do at Central State?"

"I worked as a janitor."

"For 25 years?"

"Yes."

"Did you take therapy while you were there?"

"No."

"Do you think you're going to get out of prison now?"

"Yes."

"What are you going to do when you get out?"

"Work in a factory. A foundry. There's money there. The work's dirty, hard, and heavy."

"Where do you work now?"

"In the laundry."

"What are you going to do when you get out?"

"I'll live by myself if I get out. I'll go to the show. I'll buy clothes. No one will care about me, and I'll be left alone. I'll go back to Kenosha."

"What's it like inside?"

"I have problems outside, but no one bothers me inside."

"Do you have friends inside?"

"Sure, I have some friends inside that I get along with."

"How about your friends who have left?"

"I got no contacts with those who have left."

THE ECONOMIC VIEW

I really don't know what can be said about Steve Urban. One would like to have met him before his 28 years of incarceration. His record indicates that when he first went to Waupun he was very unruly. He just plain didn't like being locked up. One also wonders what went on during his 25 years at Central State. I really

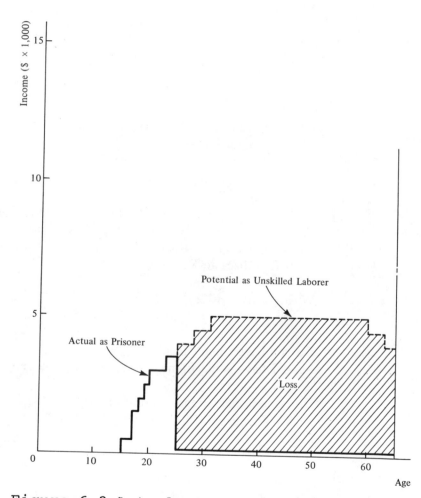

Figure 6.2 Actual Potential Earnings
Profiles - Steve Urban

can't imagine anyone emerging from an experience like that in anything but a completely deranged condition.

I doubt if Steve would ever have set the world on fire either figuratively or literally. But I have a hunch that he could have led a reasonably satisfying life doing the kind of heavy dirty jobs that most of us won't touch. The income profile I used to describe his hypothetical nonimprisoned career indicates that sort of earnings with top wages at $5,000 per year (see Figure 6.2.) The prison costs included are those of the state prison. In actual fact, Steve has spent most of his prison life in the state hospital where the costs perman are more than double those of Waupun.

The numbers in this case come out as follows:

(−) Value of Potential Earnings Without Prison	$39,783
(+) Value of Actual Earnings	14,578
(−) Value of Prison Expenses	26,840
Net Cost Valued at Age 16	$52,115

What will society do with Steve if he is let out? Don't ask me, for God's sake! It will take some pretty shrewd analysis to figure out if Steve can ever cut it in any kind of life beyond some kind of wall. The case does raise at least two very important questions, however. First of all, *if* Steve is likely to create more violence, then some kind of institutionalization is probably required for all our sakes and his as well. There are people in society who are sufficiently dangerous to require some kind of separation and, hopefully, treatment. But this raises the second question. Do the prisons of today offer the best method for handling such cases? And even if they do, must we waste the productive potential of the men within the walls on an industry that is so inefficient that it makes almost a zero return for those who provide the sweat?

CASE HISTORY: RANDY SCOTT

Randy Scott is black. He talked mostly about the prison and what it was like as an institution. He talked less about himself and was pretty well convinced that he didn't belong inside.

Randy entered Waupun on February 19, 1971, for a five-year term for the sale of marijuana. His sale was of three five-dollar bags. He is in prison, he feels, because a deal was made with the judge by his defense attorney who was a public defender; he was trapped, and there was nothing he could do. The law for which Randy was sent to prison for five years was changed a month after he was sentenced; now the maximum sentence for a first-offense marijuana sale is one year in prison.

Randy had a record before he was charged with the sale of marijuana. He was sent to Wales Reformatory when he was 16 for truancy. He was then sent to Green Bay Reformatory for nine months, and was paroled until he was 21. He went "joy riding" in a car which was not his and had his parole revoked.

Randy had a family on the outside. He was engaged to a girl and had a daughter. But now he can't reach his fiancee. He said, "She let me down. But I don't care. If I see her when I get out, then 'Boom'! I'll see how I feel when I get out and see her. Maybe I'll overlook it."

Randy worked when he was on the outside as an auto painter, a model, and a musician in a band. He got a job at A. O. Smith by lying about his prison record; but they found out, and he was fired. When he gets out this time, he wants to go into broadcasting or into music at the University of Wisconsin—Milwaukee. Randy's prison work is as director of the prison radio station, which is a very difficult position because you can never please everyone all the time by the music you play or the kinds of news you broadcast. But he is handling it extremely well.

Randy has some good things to say about the prison. While he has been there, he has been able to go to school. He has gotten his high school diploma and has taken some college English. But he doesn't like the trade courses that are offered. He particularly doesn't like the welding course because of the petty rules and regulations within it.

What Randy really worries about is the effect the prison itself has on the inmates, because of its very nature and because of the type of therapy and rehabilitation offered. His major concern is with security. According to Randy, the whole security mechanism of a prison downgrades a man. If you have to go to the hospital in Madison, you are handcuffed as you walk down the hall and that "drops your pride." The nurses are not allowed to talk to you even if they want to. They lock your door, and the guards listen to everything that you say. Said Randy: "There you are in a bed with an infected leg, and you can't even walk; and they have locked your door and have a guard on it, and no one can speak to you."

He went on: "As for the prison itself, there are more petty rules here at Waupun than there were in Green Bay; and there are more petty officers as well. You can get a 'report' for being out of your area, for going to the bathroom without permission, or for taking an extra pat of butter at meal time." He added that at meals you are allowed to have as much food as you want; but you may not go back for seconds, and you must eat all that you have taken on your tray.

With regard to rehabilitation, Randy had already talked about the fact that the educational facilities were good for what he needed but that the trade courses were not. His particular concern, however, was the rehabilitative therapy which was given. As he put it, "The psychiatrists here send all their problems to Central State Hospital, and they come back as vegetables . . ." He added that the social workers, whom he basically liked, had very little power because they had to go through security for everything they wanted to do. It was Randy's feeling that either the therapists couldn't do anything, as was the case with the social workers, or they didn't do anything, as was the case with the psychiatrists, who tended to send their serious problems away and didn't deal with the minor problems.

According to Randy, a prison record was going to be a "stone around your neck," and there was no way to avoid it. When you got out, life was going to be rough. And Randy couldn't understand why people were sent to prison at all.

"What effect," he asked, "could sending someone to prison for a first offense of armed robbery have? There could certainly not be a good effect on that first offender. It makes him bitter. Armed robbery should be a crime where you are sentenced to a halfway house. The really violent types should be sent to prison and should be put under maximum security, because if they are violent outside, they're going to be violent inside too, and the other inmates have to be protected. But if they're not violent, what good does it do to send them to prison? I know lifers here who wouldn't hurt a grape."

Randy wants to go to the boys' school and tell them to stay out of Waupun. And on being black in prison, Randy said, "Blacks are categorized by farmers on the staff who know about blacks only through TV."

THE ECONOMIC VIEW

In this case, I make no pretense of maintaining any kind of objectivity. This one is really incredible! A 16-year-old kid is sent to the boys' school for *truancy*. This in itself is unbelievable. And when he gets there, they decide he's too old for the boys' school and transfer him (without further hearing or appeal) to the *prison* at Green Bay. It's called a reformatory; but, man, it's a rough and tough prison any way you cut it. Again, it's an excellent preparatory school for any of the excellent job opportunities available upon graduation in the fields of theft, dope peddling, etc. Well, the "borrowed car" incident was about as predictable as anything could be. The only strange thing was that the offense wasn't more serious. But now we get to the big time—a five-year sentence at our maximum security institution for the sale of three five-dollar bags of grass.

Both Frank and I are betting that Randy is going to make it in spite of the rimming his background and our culture has given him thus far. A look at his earnings profiles in Figure 6.3 shows you my bet. Randy will get out soon, and I hope he will come to our university. I suspect he will become involved in some of the new programs of community education that are developing. Since these are not the most remunerative jobs in the world, I have reduced the estimate of maximum annual earnings to $11,000 instead of the $16,000 used for other college graduates. Randy's case is the least expensive in terms of forgone product of any thus far used in the illustrations. If he had not had many of his experiences, I doubt if he would ever have gone to college or done particularly well in the workaday world. But I'm damn sure he will make it now. For everyone's sake, I hope so.

The numbers in this case come out as follows:

(−) Value of Potential Earnings Without Prison	$57,828
(+) Value of Actual Earnings	49,128
(−) Value of Prison Expenses	11,832
Net Cost Valued at Age 16	$20,532

The numbers just presented for the three people from Waupun are nothing more than reasonable estimates. In no way do they

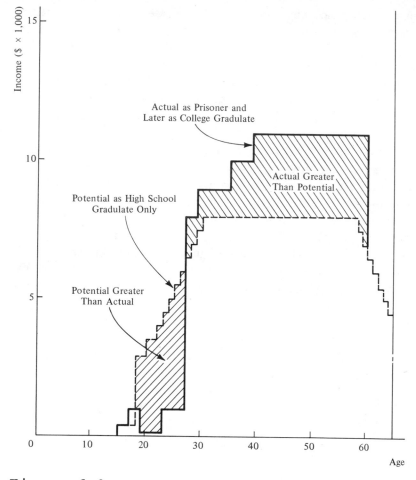

Figure 6.3 Actual and Potential Earnings
Profiles - Randy Scott

represent a careful analysis of all of the ramifications of crime and punishment. There are no estimates of the externalities imposed on the families and friends of either victims or perpetrators. But, hopefully, as rough as my estimates are, you may get some idea of the magnitudes involved. Ask a prisoner about time. Most of them can tell you just how many months and days they have been in and expect to remain. Time is a very expensive commodity, particularly for mortal man. The compound interest calculations merely illustrate this eternal fact.

Postscript

THERE are a few summary points that should be restated before closing this little exercise. Crime, any crime, is very expensive to all concerned, *unless* you are clever enough or big enough to get away with it. Then it can obviously be a very worthwhile occupation. Because crime is potentially expensive, society should look carefully at all of the activities it has made illegal. If society wishes to use the law to impose morality rather than just to prevent the imposition of external costs, then society had better look carefully at the costs it will impose on itself.

Basically, we are providing the primary support for organized criminal activity by making drugs, gambling, and, to a much lesser extent, sex illegal. By creating this basic support for the mob, we indirectly create the network that provides the all important middleman and support services for crimes against property.

The guillotine was not designed to chop up the trunk of a human being, but rather the vulnerable, slender, and more easily severable neck. If we really want to go after the property crime problem, we should go for the throat! Get the big guys in the middle of the distribution chain and the little guys at both ends will be peanuts. I really wonder what would happen if the FBI took most of the resources it spends hunting long-haired "hippie-commie freaks" and *really* went after the mob. It's an interesting idea, particularly if the mob couldn't make big money anymore because its pet projects were legalized.

We've done a lot of talking about costs and about how we should raise the cost of criminal activity. This can be done by increasing the likelihood of apprehension or (perhaps) by increasing the severity of the penalties. But there is one cost I really would love to see raised to the point where no potential criminal in his right mind would ever consider a criminal career. The cost I have in mind is the criminal's *opportunity cost*. If only we could make the available earning alternatives sufficiently good, most crimes would never take place.

"Yeah, sure," you say. "Now you're telling us that crime is just another one of those things tied up with poverty and discrimination and inner cities and suburban indifference and all the rest of that stuff!" That's right.

When the kinds of scarcity that faced most of mankind involved choices between two meals versus one or none, or a coat versus a pair of shoes, I think one could have predicted that crime, particularly property crime, was inevitable—and so it was. But now we are approaching levels of material prosperity which should somehow give us the resources to attack these basic issues that have plagued man since the beginning of time as we know it.

As always, we've got some choices to make. We *can* hire more cops, give them bigger guns, give up more of our sovereignty to a police bureaucracy, build bigger prisons with thicker walls, and build more efficient electric chairs that will kill with fewer kilowatt hours of juice. We can continue to subsidize organized criminality in the name of moral righteousness, or ignore them because they are nothing more than entrepreneurs in a free market system—and damned successful ones at that!

But we can also seize the opportunity provided by our incredible technological development. We can attack pollution of the environment, including the pollution of our society created by the kinds of illegal activities that impose substantial costs on us all. Maybe the resources should go into the storefront outreach operations of our urban universities. Maybe we ought to do more *listening* to the Panthers or Angela Davis. Nobody, least of all me, would suggest that they are "right" in their views. But, brother, their views are with us, and are part and parcel of the problem. When you look at even the most superficial costs of crime, the conclusion must be that we indeed can no longer afford to do as little as we are doing now.

Crime pays, and pays well. *That* is the problem.

Appendix:

Basic Tools and Concepts

FOR a long time, the world has dubbed economics as the "dismal science." Probably one reason for its dubious reputation is the fact that many economics courses are duller than a ten-year prison stretch. But the primary reason for the bad name is that economists deal with a dismal fact of life that doesn't seem to change much as civilization marches on through time. For some reason or other, mankind always seems to want more than is available. At very primitive levels of existence, wants take the form of more food, more clothing, or more shelter. But even in societies where most men have been able to satisfy these basics, other wants spring up. Men the world over appear to be damned to a life of *scarcity*. That's the dirty word that brands economics as the dismal science.

We all know what scarcity is all about, right? Well, maybe. In order to keep their place in the world of academic snobbery, economists, like other witch doctors, develop a language all their own. They take perfectly good words that everyone knows the meaning of and define them so precisely that the words lose any mystic appeal they might have had. Then they insist that everyone using the words must attach precisely the same significance to them. Our first example of this strange behavior comes when we use the word "scarcity." As far as economists are concerned, something is scarce when (1) it is desired by man, and (2) when man is willing, able, and required by conditions to give up something else to get it. Let's look at some examples.

Say you're up in the God's country of northern Michigan. If you take a deep breath of air when you get up in the morning, that breath of air will sustain you for a brief period of time. Without the air (or some other chemical substitute), you would quickly perish. Clearly, the air is yielding a positive service—a productive service—to you. And because it is useful and productive, it is considered a *good*. But unless you paid a small fortune to vacation in that part of the world, that breath of air is *not* scarce to you at that moment in time and space. You do not have to *give up* anything to enjoy that magnificent lungful of atmosphere. In a strict sense, of course, breathing requires energy which we get from food. Since food is generally scarce, the act of breathing is not completely free. But, basically, the air for you at that moment is a *free good*.

Now let's say that you become a fresh air addict, but that to keep body and soul together you must live and work in the city of Detroit. There's a problem! True, you can breathe the polluted stuff downtown and survive at least most of the time. But if you want *fresh* air, you'll have to give up some other resource to purify the junk and bring it closer to its northern Michigan counterpart. At this stage of the game, *fresh* air becomes scarce—therefore, it becomes an *economic good*.

Carry the example one step farther. In a moon capsule, some type of air or close atmospheric substitute is required to sustain life. I wouldn't even attempt to guess the cost per cubic foot of the "air," but I'm sure it would buy a lot of air conditioning in downtown Detroit. Notice that physiologically the air is performing pretty much the same function in all three cases. But in one instance, the good can be obtained without giving up anything else. In the other two cases, use of the air requires giving up some alternative good or resource.

One of the seeming paradoxes of increased productivity is that while it may well reduce scarcity in some sense of the word, it can enlarge the *economic problem*. Increased productivity increases the alternatives available to individuals, and thus it can increase the need for choice between those alternatives. It is this business of choice that is the meat of economic study. How and with what results do people make decisions between viable alternatives?

OPPORTUNITY COST

Might not the whole problem of scarcity be eliminated if we are at some time able to produce goods and services for little or no human effort? If usable energy becomes extremely cheap, won't that reduce scarcity to a negligible problem? The answer is that at least until we are able to control, create, and eliminate *time*, scarcity will remain with us. We can end up with free automobiles, free hair cuts, free trips to the moon or to Disneyland; but as long as individuals prefer living to dying, *time* will remain scarce. A belief in eternal life reduces the severity of this scarcity, but it does not eliminate it. "Free time"—like the proverbial "free lunch"—just doesn't exist. In fact, as material consumption choices expand, time becomes more and more the limiting and ultimate scarcity. To use our material bounty and gain satisfaction or utility from it, man must expend his limited time. You can get a new sailboat; but if you are to gain any pleasure (other than pride of ownership) from it, time must be expended.

As man's productivity increases, he can, of course, gain leisure time. This will tend to reduce the time constraint, but it will never eliminate it. A moment today is not identical with a moment tomorrow. To use a moment of time today for any given purpose means that some other alternative use is automatically forgone. The economist again starts generating jargon and calls these alternatives that are forgone "opportunity costs." Opportunity costs consist of *anything*, material or ethereal, physiological or psychological, that is given up to get something else or to take an alternative course of action. When anything is *scarce*, an opportunity cost is generated by acquiring it.

As we have said, time is the ultimate constraint on man. But there are also constraints that limit the material choices available to most of us. With few exceptions, we would prefer at least a bit more money than we have now. More money gives us a generalized ability to command more goods and services. It expands the available choice sets. Of course, nothing requires us to spend additional money. In fact, if having more money happens to bother us, all we need to do is to give it away. Believe me, there will be plenty of takers! So again, for most of us, our money—or, more generally, our material wealth and income—sets the limit or *constraint* on our available choices and behavior in a wide range of material activity. In a market economy, this wealth and income is the result either of productive effort within the system, inheritance from forebears, gifts and transfers from others, or a special kind of transfer generated by "illegal" activity.

THE LAW AND ECONOMICS

This last category brings up another kind of constraint which limits people's choice sets—the law. The laws of a society set forth the "rules of the game." They set the limits on individual behavior that the power holders in the community feel are appropriate. Ideally, in a society that highly values individual freedom of action, the rules of the game only limit the kind of action which would create the unreimbursed external costs described earlier. Thus, beating your neighbor (physically) is usually illegal. Stealing your neighbor's car is looked upon with some concern. In other societies, the constraints of the law may be considerably broader and include costs imposed for such things as criticizing the leadership or not meeting production goals. Whatever laws exist—"good" or "bad"—they all act to constrain human behavior according to the government's wishes and are enforced through some type of police action.

The enactment and enforcement of laws is the result of calculating some kind of cost/benefit analysis. Those in power decide that a proposed law will result in greater benefits to them or their constituents than the costs of having it. The costs consist of reductions in personal freedom and the obvious expense of enforcing the law. Take an earlier example: suppose the U.S. government makes it a federal offense for me to kick my boss? This law imposes a cost on me by limiting what otherwise would be a personally desirable action. But the governing body decides that the benefit to society of limiting this type of behavior clearly exceeds *both* the cost to my personal freedom (or to others who would like to kick him, too) and the cost of enforcing the anti-boss-kicking law. Notice that this generalization about the cost/benefits of enacting and enforcing laws has nothing to do with the actual kind of society under consideration. In a pure dictatorship, where the leader makes all the rules, the same kind of calculus takes place before establishing the rule. In this case, of course, the cost and benefits are perceived by the leader himself rather than by the broader opinion base that exists in a pluralist society.

PROPERTY RIGHTS

The economic problem of scarcity exists. No slogan, system, or wishful thought will eliminate it. But with or without conscious effort, the problem will be "solved"; somebody or some group is going to end up with the scarce item, and somebody else is going to go without. It is the job of any economic *system* to provide the machinery for allocating the scarce items. But we still have one more basic concept to look at before talking about systems.

The first step that is essential in even talking about allocating scarce items is the establishment of *rights* over these items. Property rights must be established and enforced before the society can take on the problem of either production of distribution. This is not to say that a system of *private* property rights must be established, but merely that some person or body must have the right to determine how a scarce item is to be used, who is to use it, and what the necessary ingredients for exchange are to be. It's probably worthwhile to stop for a moment and look at a world where property rights are destroyed in order to gain insight into the magnitude of the problem.

Imagine that tomorrow morning you wake up and turn on the morning news only to find our fearless leader, President Freeloader, staring out of the tube. It turns out that Freeloader has been listening to his economic advisors, whose economic nonsense has led them to come up with a simple solution to the problems of hunger and malnutrition in the country. Effective immediately, all foodstuffs in the country will belong to all the people. Nobody, including the government itself, will be allowed to establish any rights over any existing foodstuffs nor any food produced in the future. Everything will belong to everybody. Food has just been made a *free good*. No one has to give up anything to obtain any item of edible goods. Given this situation, let your imagination run a little. First of all, while the law now says that food is a free good, it really isn't. At a zero price, there will be a greater quantity of food demanded than there is available.

Obviously, the first thing to do is rush to the local supermarket. The doors are now open to everyone, and the owner has shot himself. Nobody really cares much about this last fact since the bum has been exploiting the customers for years. The place is already jammed. All the good cuts of meat have disappeared, but there is a little fat hamburger left. All the high quality frozen foods are gone, but there are some cheap canned vegetables which you throw into the shopping cart. As you're leaving the store, somebody who came in even later than you did spots the hamburger in your shopping cart and grabs it. "Hey," say you, "that's mine! Give it back!"

"Who says it's yours?" comes the reply. "You've got no more right to that hamburger than I do." You slug the sneak thief and call in a cop from outside to arrest him. But there's a problem. The cop arrests you for assault and battery. You protest bitterly that you were only protecting your rights to the meat. But you had forgotten. As of 8:00 A.M., you *had* no rights to the meat. The only rights you have now are those that you can enforce yourself without breaking some other law—like assault. Oh well! You apologize and the cop lets you off. On the trip back home, you cool down a little and decide to get to the store earlier tomorrow when the resupply trucks arrive.

At home, disaster has struck. The quality of the contents of your wine cellar was a well-known legend—well enough known so that someone has broken into the house and swiped all the wine except one lousy bottle of Christian Brothers Rosé. As you arrive, the last thief is just leaving with four bottles under each arm. Call the fuzz! Since the thief is a little fellow, you manage to hold him until the boys in blue arrive. But again, you've forgotten. The wine is as much his as yours. But how about the breaking and entering into your house? Sorry, Charlie, you have no right to keep people away from your foodstuffs, including the wine.

The next day the problem becomes even greater. Since the supermarkets are now ''giving away'' their food, there is absolutely no incentive for them to restock—and, of course, they don't. Food throughout the distribution chain has also been made ''free,'' and the warehouses around the country have been stripped of all perishables such as meat and dairy products. There are still ample stocks of lower quality items such as off-brand canned goods and grain staples. However, it will only be a matter of days before everyone realizes the most bitter fact of life in the whole business. Unless something changes and changes drastically, there will be no more food produced. Why would anyone be foolish enough to produce it? The answer you might give is that people would start producing for their own use just to keep alive. Maybe. But remember that once the food is grown, there is nothing to prevent others from getting into your garden and cleaning house. In fact, the law which has made food a free good *protects* precisely that kind of action.

In spite of the law, however, food hasn't really become a free good. The tendency for people to establish property rights over something that is economically scarce has required the government to expend resources to prevent that behavior. So, the cops have been used to keep people from establishing rights over foodstuffs. An analogy can be found in the fact that part of the national park rangers' job is to prevent the takeover of park lands by squatters. They are to keep land that is supposedly free to all the people from being made the private domain of one individual or group. If there were sufficient land so that no two people would want the same piece, this wouldn't be necessary. But because land is economically scarce, free lands will have to be protected to keep them free. The minute this happens, resources are involved in the policing action; then, of course, the good can no longer be considered free. To some *individuals,* it may be free; but to society as a whole, it isn't.

How do we get out of this dilemma? Some might come up with the simplest solution of all. Let the government take over all food production and distribution. That would certainly straighten things out in a hurry! Sorry, folks, that solution is against the rules. Once the government takes over food, property rights are reestablished. The government has these rights, true enough; but now property rights are back with us whether we like it or not.

What happens if we destroy the "pig" government and let people become truly free—free of all the oppressive laws that shackle men's minds and freedom of action? Why not anarchy? Actually, anarchy will work just fine until one person's actions start to interfere with another person's actions. Then the fur is going to start flying. Notice that as long as only free goods are involved, there will, by definition, be no conflict. But when economic goods are involved, there must be some allocation mechanism to determine who is going to end up with the goodies and who is going to go without. In the absence of any government, this process will revert back to the oldest (and perhaps the most effective) allocation mechanism known to man. He who can capture and defend his control over something gets it. He who can't, loses. We'll be back in the jungle in a literal sense.

So what does all this mean? Quite simply, scarcity exists because man *thinks* he wants something in greater quantities than are readily available without cost. It is perfectly true that one way to eliminate scarcity is to change the nature of man in such a way that he no longer *desires* material goods. For that matter, maybe we can change him so that he doesn't even desire more time. That's possible; and, in fact, many cultures have approached the solution of scarcity in precisely that way. Through religious or other moral strictures, consumption for personal satisfaction *in this life* has been frowned upon; only the very minimum requirements to sustain life have been considered "right." In the time department, the whole concept of eternal life—a continuing existence beyond this mortal vale—is an attempt to reduce the importance, desirability, and scarcity of time in the present.

If scarcity can be solved by this simple expedient, why do we go through the seemingly endless hassle of attempting to solve it by increasing productivity? This is where the economist passes the buck to the psychologist, theologist, or moral philosopher. From casual observation, however, one can conclude that *most* societies which have had the *chance* to increase their material standard of living have done so. For valid reasons or not, most men seek to increase their creature comforts. It is on the assumption that this premise is *true* rather than *right* that this presentation is based. Perhaps the nature of man can be changed. Fine! In the meantime, the problems of man, the present beast, must be faced if we are to have the time to develop into man, the more perfect being.

GOODS AND CONSTRAINTS

For economic purposes, all things in the universe can be split into those which have some effect on man at some point in time from those which do not or will not impinge on man. Things which will impinge on man, we call *goods*. The rest of the universe, we call *nongoods*. Obviously, this breakdown will change over time. Some star a billion light years away may have no meaning for man today, but that situation could conceivably change in the next few generations.

In Figure A.1, a universe consisting of everything broken into either goods or nongoods is shown. But since nongoods are not our concern in this study, goods are further broken down into those which yield a desirable service (positive goods) and those which yield disservice (negative goods). Positive goods are those which at least someone desires, while negative goods include such things as pollution and crime. While we may like or dislike something,

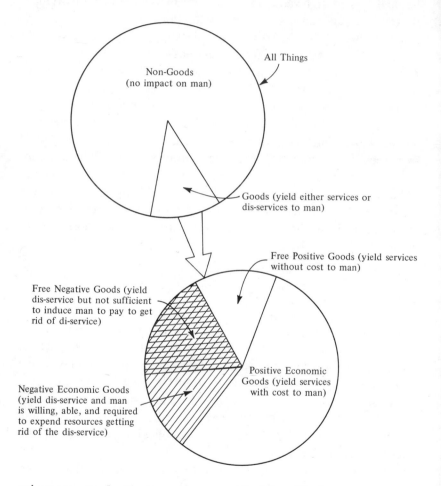

Figure A.1 Economics and the Universe

the degree of that like or dislike will determine whether the good is *free* or *economic*. If it is something on which we are willing, able, and required to expend other resources, then it is an *economic good*. If this is not the case, then it is a *free good*.

Examples of free and economic goods that yield positive services have already been covered, but free and economic *negative goods* may be something new to you. If you are breathing some air with a small amount of crud in it, the crud is yielding a disservice to you. However, the disservice is sufficiently small so that you are unwilling to expend any resources to clean it up. This is a free negative good. When you start talking about pollution, which people *are* willing to pay something to get rid of, then the negative good becomes *economic* instead of *free*.

Petty crime is another example of a free negative good. Those affected don't like it, but they are unwilling to pay the resources needed to stop the activity. On the other hand, major crime is something on which many people are willing to expend resources. Here we have a negative economic good again.

The idea of a constraint can be shown in many different ways, one of which is illustrated in Figure A.2. In this case, I have chosen a hypothetical situation in which I could give one full academic year either to writing "scholarly" articles or to teaching. If I do the former, I can write six articles but do no teaching. Time is my constraint. If, on the other hand, I use all of my working time for teaching, I can teach eight economics courses in the two semesters. And for every economics course I teach, I will have to give up writing some constant quantity of articles. In other words, every economics course I teach will *cost* me some quantity of article writing. As long as the cost remains the same for any combination of the two activities, I can easily calculate what that cost is. Resourcewise, six articles are equivalent to eight courses or

6 A = 8 C. Therefore, the cost of one article is
A = 8/6 C or 1 1/3 course per article written.

That means that for every article I write, I will be unable to teach

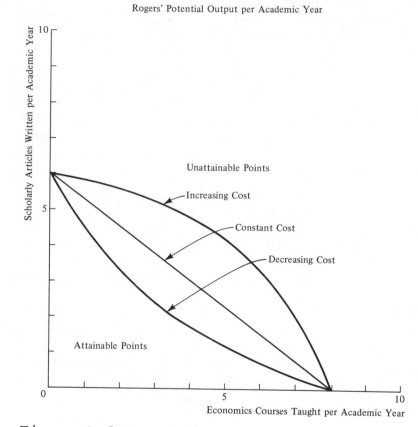

Figure A.2 Constraint and Cost

1 1/3 economics courses. The cost of teaching courses can be calculated in a similar way:

8 C = 6 A or the cost of C = 6/8 A or 3/4
   articles per course taught.

The straight line in Figure A.2 illustrates this constant cost case. The line itself represents the boundary between choices that are attainable and those that are not. It is a production possibilities boundary. Points downward to the left of the line can be accomplished, although my time would not be fully employed. Points upward to the right on the other hand, are impossible given the time constraint and my productivity in each endeavor.

The business of *opportunity costs* is also made clear by this tool. The costs described above are, in fact, opportunity costs. The cost of teaching one economics course is the forgone opportunity of writing 3/4 of an article. The cost of writing one article is the forgone opportunity of teaching 1 1/3 economics courses.

SPECIALIZATION AND TRADE

Why in the name of God don't people keep out of each other's hair, do their own thing, and eliminate all the troubles that pop up when a man starts to interact with other men? Wow, would that ever simplify things! No more wars over territory! No more fights to gain "economic advantage!" Beautiful! All that would be left to fight about is love. To see why man doesn't go this route, let the imagination roam once again.

Let's say that President Freeloader was so impressed by the success of his free food idea that he decided to try another economic miracle. He reasoned that if most fights had their roots in economic issues, the solution was to eliminate any economic interaction between men. This seemed simple enough. All that needed to be done was to make any kind of trade or exchange between two or more people illegal. Anybody caught performing such trades or exchanges would have their heads chopped off.

The next morning Joe Bluecollar arrived at the factory and found he didn't have a job. Sylvia Whitecollar arrived for work and found she didn't have job either. Charles Fatcat went to the office, but once he was there realized that there was nothing to do—at least nothing that would put bread on the table that night. In one simple action—eliminating exchange—the entire interdependent economic system came to a screeching halt.

Those people on the land, the farmers, were comparatively well off. They quickly converted their heating plants to wood fuel, dug out kerosene lamps from the attic, and saved all the fuel oil remaining in their heating plant tanks for future light. Those farmers who were still dumb enough to be generalists in that they raised a mixed bag of products for their own use, as well as for sale, were in good shape. They already had the basic necessities to support life—their own life.

But anyone, farmer or industrialist, who did not have the wherewithall to start a subsistence operation independent of all others was soon in trouble. All energy sources which depended on specialized labor and equipment were cut off within a few days. Some people in the cities planted window boxes, but this effort at food production was pitifully small and the leadtime would have starved them out anyway. Concrete sidewalks and streets were quickly ripped up in a frantic effort to find viable soil. Of course, there was no fertile soil; it had been stripped away years ago to provide footings for the concrete jungle.

The roadways themselves were almost without purpose, since all automobile traffic had ceased within days of the order. Some of the naturalists applauded as automobile exhausts died out. But these same "environmentalists" soon became even more upset as smoke from woodburning (mostly furniture and fixtures) filled the air. Sewage and garbage collected in the streets. Indoor plumbing became a joke. There was a mass exodus from the metropolitan areas in search of any plot of ground with which the individuals by their own efforts could support life.

The ultimate truth came with the incredible famine that ensued the following year. Even with the comparatively low population per acre of productive land, it was soon apparent that there were insufficient resources to support the level of population when everyone was required to produce his own material goods and services. Most people turned out to be darned poor farmers or subsistence survivors. But Mother Nature takes care of these kinds of problems; by the second year, the population had been cut down to size. Fortunately, President Freeloader and his advisors were among the first to go. It was widely rumored that their demise was from causes other than starvation, but this was never proven. Anyway, a much smaller but wiser population emerged from the experiment when trade started up again.

Nobody had realized what tremendous differences in total productivity the process of specialization made possible. Without this specialization and trade, the creation and use of machines—capital goods—was impossible, and man was doomed to perform only such tasks as his own hands and brute strength permitted. Notice that I have been using the phrase "specialization and trade" as though the two went hand in hand. They do. Without trade and exchange, specialization is impossible. If trade is inhibited, specialization will be less practical. Less specialization means less productivity, everything else being equal (which it seldom is).

When trade is possible, it means that it is no longer necessary for each person to perform all the tasks involved in making the myriad of goods desired. It also means that no matter how stupid or inefficient a person is at producing *anything*, trade holds some hope for his improvement. This simple fact of life is not necessarily obvious when you first think about it. It depends on something called *comparative advantage*, and an example of this is probably the best way to explain it.

I am an addict. I am addicted to sailboats and sailing. For some people, this activity is a sport and avocation. For me, it is my vocation; my work is my avocation. Anyway, last summer I did a very stupid thing when starting a race. (For the sailors among the readers, I puffed a flying jibe in 30 knots of winds. The boom hooked the permanent backstay, ripping out the chainplate and about one third of the transom.) In any case, there was a mess to repair. In all modesty, I am a pretty fair ship's carpenter.

I've been around boats all my life and can outperform most wood butchers when it comes to any kind of repair work. At the time of the accident, however, I was also under contract to my sadistic publisher to deliver some manuscripts by a certain date. To do so on time would have meant one amount of money. To do so late would have meant a considerably smaller sum.

Now let's compare my position with that of my potential trading partner—the wood butcher at the local boatyard. I was better than he in performing *both* the alternative occupations. Presumably, I could write the needed books better and more efficiently than he, and I could also repair the boat more quickly and effectively. Yet I chose to write the books and hire him to repair the boat. Why? Because in terms of what I would have had to forgo, it was cheaper for me to hire the repair work and write the books. Every hour that I spent working on the boat would have cost me dollars in forgone book earnings.

The purpose of this tale is not to brag about my abilities, but to show how *both* the shipwright and I gained from the ensuing trade. Because of the law of comparative advantage, nobody has to be *absolutely* the best at anything in order to gain from the specialization and trade process. The only requirement is that people possess relatively different levels of ability in performing different jobs. You don't really care what it costs *the other guy* to produce something you want as long as you can buy it from him cheaper than you can produce it yourself.

Comparative advantage can be illustrated very quickly and clearly. In Figure A.3, production possibilities constraints are shown for me and the shipwright. The numbers are arbitrary, but they illustrate the fact that I have an *absolute* advantage and he has an absolute disadvantage in both occupations. By the same token, I have a *comparative* disadvantage and he has a comparative advantage in the repair of boats.

In one year's working time, I could either repair 80 boats *or* write 1,000 pages of manuscript. During that same period, the shipwright could either repair 60 boats with the same quality *or* produce 300 pages of satisfactory manuscript. Notice that we're assuming that virtually *anyone* could write an economics textbook

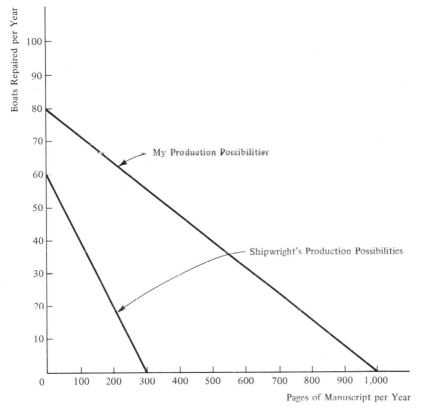

Figure A.3 Comparative Advantage

if he had to. And there's probably more truth to this assumption than most people realize. Anyway, I could clearly do either job more efficiently; but let's see what it would cost *each* of us to do *each* job ourselves.

For me,
$$80 \text{ B} = 1{,}000 \text{ M} \quad \text{where B} = \text{boat repair and}$$
$$\text{M} = \text{pages of manuscript.}$$

Therefore, the relative prices of these occupations in terms of *my* opportunity costs are

$$\text{B} = 1{,}000/80\text{M or } 12 \text{ } 1/2 \text{ M per B.}$$

For every boat I repair, I will have to forgo writing 12 1/2 pages of manuscript. Similarly, for every page of manuscript I write, it will cost me

$$\text{M} = 80/1{,}000 \text{ or } .08 \text{ of a boat repair.}$$

Now take a look at the same calculations for the shipwright. He can produce either 60 boat repairs *or* 300 pages of manuscript per working year (60 B = 300M).

For him,
$$\text{B} = 300/60\text{M or } 5 \text{ M per B.}$$

Conversely, the price of manuscripts is

$$\text{M} = 60/300 \text{ B or } .2 \text{ of a boat repair.}$$

Now the comparative advantage becomes clear. For me to repair the boat, I must give up 12 1/2 pages of manuscript. The shipwright only forgoes the production of five pages for the same repair job. Conversely, I would forgo only .08 of a boat repair for every page of manuscript I wrote. But the shipwright would forgo .2 of a repair for every page he wrote. Therefore, *in terms of our own alternative costs,* we can trade cheaper if we each do our *own thing* than we can if we produce some of both products.

SYSTEMS FOR ALLOCATING GOODS

So far we have discussed economic concepts and axioms that have very little to do with the kinds of systems society actually uses in allocating goods. There are several systems, all of which work to some degree or other. The first of these is undoubtedly the oldest, and it survives today as a viable way of distributing economic goods. It depends on no organized society or legal structure, although many times such a structure reinforces the tenets of the system. I'm referring to allocation by force—the "capture and protect" system. This has already been discussed briefly. Basically, the idea is for some individual or group to grab as much as possible, establish rights over the booty, and then protect those rights from interlopers—by force if necessary. At this stage of the game, we aren't discussing the "goodness" or "fairness" of any particular system, but merely whether it is capable of allocating some item which is not costless. This system *can* handle the problem very nicely. It tends to produce a society in which the strong get stronger and the weak get only as strong as they are allowed to.

Over time, this system can develop into something called a hierarchical system in which the leaders or strongmen are institutionalized so that leadership and economic decision-making become functions of birth and lineage. In such a system, the allocation patterns themselves become traditionalized. In the Middle Ages, for example, serfs were supposed to eat bread made from the chaff of the grain while the bread made from refined flour was reserved for the lord of the manor. No one questioned this arrangement. It seemed proper because it had been done that way for generations. Again, whatever the rights and wrongs of the system, it certainly relieved a lot of pressure on scarce resources.

A comparatively modern outgrowth of the strongman systems

involves the planning of allocation by a central body. This planning may cover only certain major items in the economy, such as steel, oil, or heavy industry. But it may also cover virtually all allocation decisions, including consumer goods of all kinds. The makeup and power base of the planning body can be as varied as the society. It can range from a group which has seized power by force to a group which has been elected by free vote of the individuals in the community. It can use an estimate of what people in the economy want, or it can attempt to ignore this factor and satisfy other goals, such as capital development or the building up of a war machine.

The business of popular support is very important, however, in any planned economy. Without it, the costs of enforcing the planning decisions can become prohibitive. When plans involving material goods and services are implemented against the will of a large portion of any population, the costs of enforcing those plans will rise to prohibitive proportions in short order. Revolutionary societies are well aware of this fact of life and use "revolutionary fervor" as a conscious tool in getting the populace to go along with otherwise unpopular short-run allocation decisions. Giving up consumption is a much easier idea to sell if those who are doing the giving up can be convinced of a future place in heaven, a seat on the revolutionary council, or bread in the bellies of their children. This support or lack of it is an important factor in our present subject—crime.

The last system we will consider is the market. Virtually all economic systems use the market to some degree. This is true for the most dedicated socialist or communist states, as well as for the so-called capitalistic cultures of the western world. Basically, the market weighs the desires and abilities of potential suppliers of the good. Of course, there may be outside influences —such as the actions of governments, power groups like big business and big unions, or even consumer pressure groups—that impinge on the market interaction.

A market operating without any significant concentrated pressure is called a "free" or "competitive" market. One common misconception is that a market must be free in order to perform the allocation process. This is absolutely not true. To accomplish allocation and arrive at certain optimal solutions, such freedom must exist. Notice, however, that "optimal" in this case is based on some value judgments; it means that no one can be made "better off" without making someone else "worse off."

The free market allows people to trade. By definition, trade is something that is carried out voluntarily between two or more partners. If *exchange* is coerced, it is no longer *trade* but rather expropriation of some sort. Therefore, when trade occurs, *both* partners must be gaining something or the exchange just wouldn't take place. True, one partner may gain more than the other by somebody's standards; nevertheless, a trade implies some gain to both—or all—parties to it. Market operations are the mechanism by which trade is carried out.

The market used to be a place in which buyers and sellers of similar products gathered, haggled, and arranged exchange either on a goods-for-goods basis (barter) or by using something called money. In one sense, money is merely a special kind of good which like any other, provides a flow of useful services. However, unlike any other good, money also provides a *medium of exchange*—a way of carrying out exchange without actually transferring nonmoney goods for other nonmoney goods. It also serves as a *store of value*. And in this function, money shares its services with many other goods, including stocks and bonds, land, capital goods of various kinds, and even people as holders of productive skills.

MARKETS—DEMAND

When looking at a market phenomenon, the first thing that is usually done is to separate the forces that affect the *demand* for the product from the forces that influence the *supply* of the good. *Demand* refers to the quantities of a good that people will be willing and able to pay for at different prices. In other words, demand is a whole series of *prices* and *quantities demanded,* when everything else that might affect the quantity demanded of the good is held constant.

What are the other factors that would influence the quantity of something that people would be willing and able to purchase? Let's take beer for an example. At any moment in time, the higher the price of beer, the smaller the quantity of beer I would demand. When I say this, I am merely illustrating the *law of demand*. As the price of something goes higher, the quantity of it demanded will fall; conversely, as the price of the item falls, the quantity demanded will rise. If the change in quantity demanded is very great with a comparatively small change in price, the demand for the good is said to be *elastic*. If quantity demanded is comparatively insensitive to changes in price, the demand is said to be *inelastic*.

When we talk about other factors having an influence on the quantity of a good demanded, we are talking about a *change in demand*—a change in the entire schedule of prices and quantities demanded of the good. In the beer example, beer and whiskey are partial substitutes for me. On most occasions, however, I prefer whiskey to beer. Now, if the price of whiskey went down considerably, what do you think I would do? I *know* what I would do. My consumption of beer would fall, and my consumption of whiskey would rise—everything else being equal. In other words, the lower whiskey prices would decrease the quantity of beer I would demand. My *demand* for beer would fall because of the *cheaper price* of a reasonably close substitute.

Take another example of the change in price of a *related good*. Like many people, I eat pretzels when I drink beer. Beer and pretzels are complementary goods as far as I'm concerned. What will happen to the *demand* for beer if the *price* of a *complementary good*—pretzels—goes down? This will make consumption of the package (beer and pretzels) cheaper. Since consuming the package is cheaper, one would expect that the demand for the given good would *rise* with the *fall* in the price of some complementary good. And so it would. In the beer market, the whole series of prices and quantities demanded would increase. At any given price of beer, the quantity demanded would be greater; or for any given quantity demanded, people would be willing and able to pay a higher price.

What happens to the demand for beer if my income rises? Be careful! This one isn't quite so easy. If *my* income rises, the chances are that I will begin to consume more whiskey and less of the cheaper item, beer. If this is the case, then *for me,* beer is what we call an *inferior good.* An increase in the incomes of demanders will lead to a *decrease* in the *demand* for the good. On the other hand, for some people, this might not be the case. For them, an increase in their incomes would result in an increase in the quantities of beer demanded at various prices. In this case, beer would be considered a *normal good.* One would actually have to go out in the market and measure the effects of income on demand to be sure whether any particular good was in fact normal or inferior.

Now we come to the category of *tastes* of demanders and how this factor affects the demand for a good. Tastes include such nebulous factors as style and all the other psychic factors that influence people's preferences or lack thereof. Obviously, as the tastes for some product increase, the demand for it increases. If, all of a sudden, beer drinking becomes the "in" thing to do, then any particular price of beer will be consistent with a larger quantity demanded. In a similar way, if the taste for beer decreases, the demand for beer will also decrease.

Finally, the transactions costs associated with the market for any particular commodity will also influence the demand for the commodity. If it becomes more expensive for the demander to go through the business of acquiring the good, the demand for the product will go down. A decrease in transactions costs will have the opposite effect. Transactions costs can be broken down into three subcategories—information costs, contractual costs, and policing costs (ICP). A look at each of these three subgroupings is useful.

From the demander's viewpoint, complete and accurate information must be available about the product he is considering purchasing. Besides this information, he must also *know* what the alternative use of his resources will produce in the way of satisfying his wants. Generally, we all make transactions every day operating on information we don't even realize we have. On major purchases, we may actually spend resources getting information. We might hire a real estate broker to find a house. We might consider a subscription to *Consumer Reports* worthwhile. We might also run a wanted-to-buy ad in the classified section of the newspaper. These are all examples of very obvious information costs—resources being expended by the potential buyer to get a better idea of his alternatives. But information costs are involved in all decision-making processes. And in talking about crime, the element of information costs plays a substantial part.

The demander's contracting costs are those that he incurs when actually transferring the property rights of a good from seller to himself. The simplest purchase involves some kind of contract cost, even if it is only the time spent by seller and buyer. As with information costs, both buyers and sellers will be faced with a portion of contracting costs. And to the extent that contracting costs borne by demanders go up, the demand for the good will fall and vise versa.

Remember that the only thing exchanged in any market operation is some bundle of property rights over a good or the services produced by a good. The exchange of these rights is meaningful only if the rights themselves can be enforced both before and after the exchange. This means that the costs of *policing* property rights will enter into the demand for goods. Take an example from recent history. Vandalism and robbery increased sharply in many commercial areas of Washington D.C. during the 1960s. Many shopowners resorted to private law enforcement mechanisms, such as special police, complex alarm systems, and trained dogs. How would you expect this increase in the costs of protecting store property to influence the demand for such store property? The answer is obvious; and, in fact, a substantial decrease in the demand for shop property occurred during that period.

MARKETS—SUPPLY

What sorts of things determine the quantity of a good that potential suppliers are willing and able to supply? In this case, the superficial answer is considerably simpler than in the case of demand. In a general sense, the quantity of any good people or firms are willing and able to supply depends completely on the cost of producing that good. In this statement, the word "cost" is used in its broadest sense; and for most purposes (including ours), it is useful to break down the total cost into different categories.

The first of these costs is the price of the good itself. The price of the good represents the per unit amount a potential supplier can receive if he produces or otherwise supplies the product to the market. Therefore, the price of the good also represents the amount of money the potential supplier will *forgo* if he chooses not to supply the good. In other words, it measures the actual gain if he supplies, and the potential loss if he doesn't. His basic decision as to whether or not to supply will depend on the price of the good in question *as compared to his next best alternative use of resources.* You remember that the *law of demand* stated that as price went down, quantity demanded would rise and vise versa. There is no comparable law of supply; but for most items, as the price of the good rises, the *quantity* supplied will rise too.

A second category of costs that will affect the quantity of a good supplied is the obvious one of *costs of production.* Again, these costs will depend on the alternative uses open to the factors of production involved. As alternative uses increase and/or improve, the costs of the factors will rise. This will raise the costs of production of the given good and *decrease* the quantity that suppliers will be willing and able to produce *at any given product price.* Conversely, a reduction in the alternatives available to the factors of production will lower the costs of producing the good under consideration, and increase the quantity supplied at various product prices.

A third variable affecting costs is the *technology* employed in producing the good. Technological improvements in the production process obviously reduce the cost of making the good, thereby increasing the quantity that suppliers are willing and able to produce at any given product price. Decreases in technology don't really occur unless somehow ideas themselves are lost.

Finally, suppliers face transactions (ICP) costs. They must obtain information about prospective buyers, arrange to contract the transfer of property rights to the buyer, and bear some of the costs of policing both general and specific property rights. As with any of the other categories, increases in transactions costs will decrease supply, and decreases in transactions costs will increase supply.

Well, now you have a thumbnail sketch of supply and demand. When you combine the two in a single market, the price of the good varies to bring about a solution to the problem of scarcity. As the price goes up, more production is called forth; simultaneously, smaller quantities are demanded. As the price goes down, the quantity supplied goes down, while quantity demanded goes up. It is through this action of price on *quantity* supplied and *quantity* demanded that the scarce quantity supplied is brought into equilibrium with the excess quantity demanded.

If prices are forced above an equilibrium level, the quantity demanded will be less than the quantity supplied, and an *economic surplus* will result. Inventories will accumulate, and there will be a downward pressure on prices. As long as the price is held at a certain level, the surplus will continue. The price mechanism will no longer perform the allocation function. In this case, some kind of production or selling allotment must be imposed on suppliers to eliminate the excess quantity supplied at the artificially high price. Similarly, if the price of a good is forced too low, the quantity demanded will exceed the quantity supplied, and an *economic shortage* will come into being. Here it will be necessary to come up with some rationing device in addition to the product price in order to limit the excess demand.

THE MARKET IN PICTURE AND SYMBOL

We can take the material contained in the last few pages and put it into graph form and shorthand notation very simply. In the case of demand, the quantity of a good demanded is a function of the price of the good, the price of complements to the good, the price of substitutes for the good, the incomes of demanders, the tasts of demanders, and the transactions costs (ICP costs) facing demanders. In shorthand, this comes out to

$$q_d = f (p, p_c, p_s, i, t, ICP_d).$$

Demand is equal to the relationship between the price of a good and the quantity demanded, *everything else being equal,* or

$$q_d = f (p, p_c, p_s, i, t, ICP_d).$$

In the case of supply, the quantity supplied is a function of the price of the good, the production costs of the good, the technology available, and the transactions costs facing suppliers, or

$$q_s = f (p, C, T, ICP_s).$$

Supply is the relationship between the price of the good and the quantity supplied, *everything else being equal,* or

$$q_s = f (p, C, T, ICP_s).$$

Equilibrium occurs when the price of the product is such as to bring the quantity supplied and the quantity demanded into equality, or

$$q_s = q_d.$$

Graphically, Figure A.4. illustrates supply (SS) and demand (DD) with an equilibrium price of p_o and an equilibrium quantity

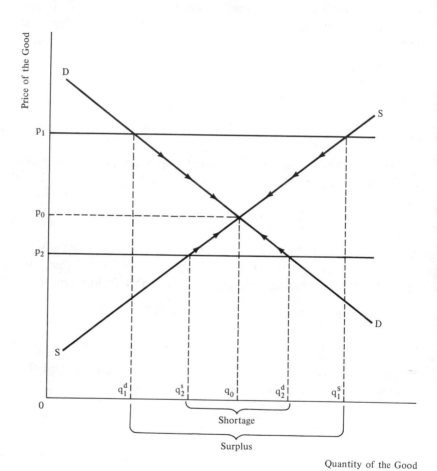

Figure A.4 The Market

of q_o. The graph also shows the forces that act on price if it is "too high" (p_1) or "too low" (p_2). If the price is too high (p_1), suppliers are overstocked and will cut their prices in an attempt to move the goods. As the price falls the quantity demanded will *increase*, the quantity supplied will *decrease*, and the surplus will reduce until it is eliminated at price p_o.

If the price is too low (p_2), quantity supplied falls to q^s_2 while quantity demanded rises to q_2d. A shortage is created. The shortage means that demanders will bid up the price, since those who want the good the most will offer to pay more than the artificially low price. This bidding process will raise the price back up toward the equilibrium level, causing quantity demanded to fall and quantity supplied to rise. Again, at price p_0, the quantity supplied and quantity demanded will be equal and forces will cease to act on price or quantity.

TIME AND VALUE

There is one more basic economic concept that is of tremendous value in gaining insight into the impact of criminal behavior. This involves the relationship between *time* and *value*.

Most men are by nature impatient. They prefer to have good things now rather than later. They also prefer to have bad things put off as long as possible. True, there are those who do not fit this mold, but most people do. One of the reasons for this general behavior involves risk and uncertainty. I know that I am hitting this letter on the typewriter. I am reasonably sure that in one minute there will be a few more words on the page. And I'm fairly certain that I will finish the Appendix this week. But every additional minute of time that goes into the future from the certainty of this moment adds an element of the unknown and uncertain. All this has led men to pay premiums for command over material goods and services in the present as opposed to waiting for command over goods and services at some future date.

People who are willing and able to forgo present command over goods and services can loan their resources to others whose demand for current goods exceeds their ability to pay. The people making these loans generally receive a fee which is called interest. Meanwhile, those who borrow command over present goods and services must pay interest. Of course, people who loan out their present resources will regain their initial command—plus the command yielded by the interest fee—when the debt is repaid. Borrowers, on the other hand, lose the temporary command gained by their borrowing when they repay the loan. In addition, they lose resources in the amount of their interest payments.

The above idea is simple and straight forward enough, but there is a less obvious corollary which is just as important. Let's say that you don't owe anyone a dime. You have no debts, and you pay cash for everything you buy. How much interest are you paying? Zero? It is perfectly true that you are not paying any out-of-pocket interest, but in terms of your alternatives—your opportunities—you are paying. Every dollar you spend represents one dollar that you *could* have invested at the current interest rate. Maybe you would starve to death if you didn't spend the dollar now, but that's not the issue. The point is that in terms of your true costs, that dollar spent is a dollar that could have earned you interest if it had been loaned out instead of used for current purchases. It may seem to you that this business of forgone opportunities—opportunity costs—comes up quite often. Well, it does—and with very good reason. Out-of-pocket costs are understood by us all, but opportunity costs are often ignored. As we look at criminal behavior in terms of economic analysis, opportunity costs are a most important part of the discussion.

How does this interest business affect the value of something now as compared to its value in the future? If I have $100 now and invest it in something that pays an annual rate of 10 percent interest, one year from now that $100 will have earned $10 interest. Therefore, the total value of my "investment" is $110. If I leave the interest as part of the loan for another year, an additional $11 of interest will be earned (10% × $110). I am now earning *compound interest*—i.e., interest on interest as well as on the original principal. The more often this compounding takes place, the greater the interest earnings. One can say, therefore, that the future value of some particular bundle of present resources is equal to its present dollar value plus any interest it can earn between now and the time in the future being discussed.

Now, let's look at the same problem from a different vantage point. Suppose that you have a stream of income coming in from some source. What is the value of that stream of income? To answer this, we must again look to the interest rate and ask, "How much money would you have to invest at the current rate of interest to earn the given stream of income?" Again, an example might help.

If Charlie is giving you $100 dollars a year and promises to do so forever and ever, how much is this income stream worth? If the going interest rate if 10 percent, then $1,000 would have to invested to earn $100 per year. The income stream, then, is *capitalized* to a principal value of $1,000. Another way of looking at it is that Uncle Charlie would have to have $1,000 loaned out at 10 percent interest in order to earn the $100 per year he is giving you.

An interesting and not altogether obvious thing happens when the interest rate goes down. How much would your $100 per year income stream be worth if the interest rate fell to 5 percent? How much would have to be invested in order to earn the $100 per year? The answer, of course, is $2,000 instead of $1,000. As the interest rate goes *down,* the capitalized value of the income stream goes *up.* Similarly, if the interest rate in the economy went from 10 percent to 20 percent per year, the capitalized value of your income stream would be cut in half. It would then be worth only $500. ($500 × 20% = $100 or $100/20% − $500).

There's one more way of asking the question; it amounts to little more than changing the arithmetic around. To get what is called the *discounted present value* of something, the question becomes, "What is the value today of something that will be worth some given value in the future?" Again, let's use an example. Say that Uncle Charlie sets up a trust which says that one year from now you will receive $100. What is the discounted *present* value of that $100? To find out, we have to determine what sum of money invested today at the current rate of interest would yield $100 of principal and interest combined at the end of one year. Assume an interest rate of 10 percent. What number multiplied by 10 percent and added to itself would yield $100? The answer, obtained by dividing $100 by 1.1 (110%) is about $90.91. When $90.91 is multiplied by 10 percent, interest in the amount of $9.09 is earned. This added to the original $90.91 equals the $100 of future value.